Pastor *and* Prayer

Three things make a divine – prayer, meditation, temptation. – Martin Luther

If you do not pray, God will probably lay you aside from your ministry as He did me, to teach you to pray. Remember Luther's maxim. "To have prayed well is to have studied well." Get your text from God, your thoughts, your words. – Robert Murray McCheyne

Recreation to the minister must be as whetting is with the mower – to be used only as is necessary for his work. Should a physician in plague time take any more relaxation or recreation than is necessary for his life, when so many are expecting his help in a case of life and death? Will you stand by and see sinners gasping under the pangs of death and say, "God does not require me to make a drudge of myself to save them"? Is this the voice of ministerial or Christian compassion or of sensual laziness and diabolical cruelty? – Richard Baxter

Squandering time is injurious to the mind. In illness I have looked back with self-reproach on days spent in my study: I was wading through history and poetry and monthly journals, but I was in my study! Another man's trifling is notorious to all observers, but what am I doing? Nothing, perhaps, that has a profit to the spiritual good of my congregation. Be much in retirement and prayer. Study the honor and glory of your master. – Richard Cecil

Pastor *and* Prayer

Why and How Pastors Ought to Pray

E. M. Bounds

We love hearing from our readers. Please contact us at www.anekopress.com/questions-comments with any questions, comments, or suggestions.

Pastor and Prayer – E. M. Bounds
Revised Edition Copyright © 2018
First edition published 1907

All rights reserved. No part of this book may be reproduced, stored in a retrieval system, or transmitted in any form or by any means – electronic, mechanical, photocopying, recording, or otherwise, without written permission from the publisher.

Scripture quotations are taken from the Jubilee Bible, copyright © 2000, 2001, 2010, 2013 by Life Sentence Publishing, Inc. Used by permission of Life Sentence Publishing, Inc., Abbotsford, Wisconsin. All rights reserved.

Cover Background: Nik Merkulov/Shutterstock

eBook and Audiobook Icons: Icons Vector/ Shutterstock, Ganibal/Shutterstock

Editors: Sheila Wilkinson and Ruth Zetek

Printed in the United States of America

Aneko Press

www.anekopress.com

Aneko Press, Life Sentence Publishing, and our logos are trademarks of

Life Sentence Publishing, Inc.
203 E. Birch Street
P.O. Box 652
Abbotsford, WI 54405

RELIGION / Christian Ministry / General

Paperback ISBN: 978-1-62245-575-1

eBook ISBN: 978-1-62245-576-8

10 9 8 7 6 5 4 3 2 1

Available where books are sold

Contents

Ch. 1: The Need for Preachers Who Pray 1
Ch. 2: Depending Solely on God 9
Ch. 3: Preaching that Kills 15
Ch. 4: Pastoral Tendencies to Be Avoided 21
Ch. 5: The Preacher's Main Business is Prayer 27
Ch. 6: What Prayer Can Do for Your Ministry 33
Ch. 7: Make Time for Prayer 39
Ch. 8: Examples of Praying Men 45
Ch. 9: Early Morning Prayer 51
Ch. 10: Devoted Prayer 55
Ch. 11: An Example of Devotion 61
Ch. 12: Preparation of the Heart 67
Ch. 13: Working from the Heart 73
Ch. 14: The Necessity of Anointing 77
Ch. 15: Anointed Preaching 81
Ch. 16: Genuine Anointing 87
Ch. 17: Spiritual Leaders Pray 93
Ch. 18: Prayer for the Preacher 99
Ch. 19: Giving Yourself to Prayer 105
Ch. 20: A Praying Pulpit Begets a Praying Pew 111
E. M. Bounds – A Short Biography 115
Similar Titles 121

Register This New Book

Benefits of Registering*

- ✓ FREE **replacements** of lost or damaged books
- ✓ FREE **audiobook** – *Pilgrim's Progress*, audiobook edition
- ✓ FREE information about new titles and other **freebies**

www.anekopress.com/new-book-registration

*See our website for requirements and limitations.

Chapter 1

The Need for Preachers Who Pray

It behooves us always to pray and not faint.
– Luke 18:1b

Study universal holiness of life. Your whole usefulness depends on this, for your sermons last only an hour or two. Your life preaches all through the week. If Satan can make a covetous minister out of a lover of praise, pleasure, and good eating, he has ruined your ministry. Give yourself to prayer and get your texts, your thoughts, and your words from God. Luther spent his best three hours in prayer.
– Robert Murray McCheyne

We constantly stretch and strain to devise new methods, new plans, and new organizations to advance and enlarge the church and secure effectiveness of the gospel. This trend of the day tends to lose sight of the man and plunge him into the plan or organization.

God's plan is to encourage and strengthen the man far more than anything else. Men are God's method.

The church is looking for better methods; God is looking for better men. *There was a man sent from God, whose name was John* (John 1:6). The dispensation that proclaimed and prepared the way for Christ was bound up in that man John. He *came for a witness, to bear witness of the Light, that all men through him might believe* (John 1:7).

Unto us a child is born, unto us a son is given. The world's salvation comes out of that cradled Son, *and the government is placed upon his shoulder, and his name shall be called The Wonderful One, The Counsellor, The God, The Mighty One, The Eternal Father, The Prince of Peace* (Isaiah 9:6). When Paul appealed to the personal character of the men who established the gospel in the world, he solved the mystery of their success.

The glory and efficiency of the gospel is dependent on the men who proclaim it. When God declares that *the eyes of the LORD run to and fro throughout the whole earth, to show himself strong in the behalf of those whose heart is perfect toward him*, he declares his dependence on men as a channel through which he exerts his power upon the world (2 Chronicles 16:9).

This vital, urgent truth is one that our industrial age is apt to forget. The forgetting of it is as deadly on the work of God as the striking of the sun from the sky would be. Darkness, confusion, and death would follow.

What the church needs today is not more and better machinery, not new organizations or more innovative methods, but men whom the Holy Spirit can use – men of prayer, men mighty in prayer. The Holy Spirit does not flow through methods, but through men. He does not show up on machinery, but on men. He does not anoint plans, but men – men of prayer.

A distinguished historian has said that the accidents of personal character are more related to the revolutions of nations than either philosophic historians or democratic politicians will admit. This truth is prominent in the gospel of Christ and in the character and conduct of the followers of Christ: Christianize the world, and you transfigure nations and individuals. Of the preachers of the gospel, this is especially true.

> The preacher makes or mars the message from God to man.

The character as well as the fortunes of the gospel are committed to the preacher. He makes or mars the message from God to man. The preacher is the golden pipe through which the divine oil flows. The pipe must not only be golden, but it must also be open and flawless, so that oil can have a full, unhindered, productive flow.

The man makes the preacher. God must make the man. If possible, the messenger is more than the message. The preacher is more than the sermon. The preacher makes the sermon. As the life-giving milk from the mother's bosom is of the mother's life, so all the words of the preacher are colored and enriched by what the preacher is. *Let your light so shine before men that they may see your good works and glorify your Father who is in the heavens* (Mathew 5:16). The treasure is in earthen vessels, and the taste of the vessel permeates and may discolor.

The man, the whole man, lies behind the sermon. Preaching is not the performance of an hour. It is the outflow of a life. It takes twenty years to make the man. The true sermon is a thing of life. The sermon grows because the man grows. The sermon is forceful because the man is forceful. The sermon is holy because the man is holy. The sermon is full of the divine anointing because the man is full of the divine anointing.

Paul termed it *my gospel*, not that he had degraded it by his personal eccentricities or diverted it by selfish appropriation, but the gospel was put into the heart and lifeblood of the man Paul, as a personal trust to be accomplished by his Pauline traits to be set aflame and empowered by the fiery energy of his fiery soul. *Now to him that is able to confirm you according to my gospel and the preaching of Jesus Christ, according to the revelation of the mystery which was concealed from times eternal* (Romans 16:25).

What were Paul's sermons? Where are they? Skeletons, scattered fragments, afloat on the sea of inspiration! But the man Paul was greater than his sermons and lives forever in full form, feature, and stature with his molding hand on the church. The preaching is but a voice. The voice dies in silence, the text is forgotten, the sermon fades from memory, but the preacher lives.

The sermon cannot rise in its life-giving forces above the man. Dead men give out dead sermons, and dead sermons kill. Everything depends on the spiritual character of the preacher. Under the Jewish dispensation, the high priest had HOLINESS UNTO THE LORD inscribed in jeweled letters on a golden frontlet (Exodus 39:30). So every preacher in Christ's ministry must be molded into and mastered by this same holy motto.

It is a crying shame for the Christian ministry to fall lower in holiness of character and holiness of aim than the Jewish priesthood. Jonathan Edwards said, "I went on with my eager pursuit after more holiness and conformity to Christ. The heaven I desired was a heaven of holiness." The gospel of Christ does not move by popular waves. It has no self-propagating power. It moves as the men who have charge of it move. The preacher must personify the gospel. He must exemplify its divine, most distinctive features. He must *be blameless, the husband of only one wife, vigilant, temperate, of worldly affections mortified, given to hospitality, apt to teach; not given to wine, not hurtful, not greedy of dishonest gain, but gentle, not contentious, not covetous* (1 Timothy 3:2-3). The constraining power of love must be in the preacher as a projecting, extraordinary, all-commanding, selfless force. The energy of self-denial must be his being – his heart and blood and bones.

The preacher must go forth as a man among men, clothed with humility, abiding in meekness, wise as a serpent, and harmless as a dove. He must demonstrate the bonds of a servant with the spirit of a king – a king in high, royal, independent bearing with the simplicity and sweetness of a child. The preacher must throw himself into his work for the salvation of men with perfect, self-emptying faith and self-consuming zeal. Hearty, heroic, compassionate, fearless martyrs must be the men who take hold of and shape a generation for God. If they are timid timeservers, position seekers, men pleasers, or men fearers, their work will be hindered. If their faith in God or his Word is weak, they cannot seize the church nor the world for God.

The preacher's sharpest and strongest preaching should be to himself. His most difficult, delicate, laborious, and thorough work must be with himself. The training of the twelve was the great, difficult, and enduring work of Christ. Preachers are not sermon makers, but men makers and saint makers, and only the one who has made himself a man and a saint is trained for this work. God does not need great talents, great learning, or great preachers, but rather, men who are great in holiness, great in faith, great in love, and great in fidelity. He wants men who are *not arrogant, not quick to anger, not given to wine, not hurtful, not greedy of dishonest gain, but a lover of hospitality, a lover of good men, temperate, just, holy, gentle, holding fast the doctrine according the faithful word* (Titus 1:7-9). God desires men who are always preaching by holy sermons in the pulpit and by holy lives out of it. These can mold a generation for God.

In this way, the early Christians were formed. Men were of a solid mold, preachers after the heavenly type – heroic, stalwart, soldierly, and saintly. For them, preaching meant self-denying, self-crucifying, serious, laborious, martyr business. They applied themselves in a way that formed in the womb a generation yet unborn for God. The preaching man is to be the praying man. As an almighty force in itself, it gives life and force to all.

The real sermon is made in the prayer closet. The man, God's man, is made in the closet. His life and his profoundest conviction were born in his secret communion with God. With the burdened and tearful agony of his spirit, he received his weightiest and sweetest messages when alone with God. Prayer makes the man; prayer makes the preacher; prayer makes the pastor.

The pulpit today is weak in praying. The pride of learning is against the dependent humility of prayer. Prayer in the pulpit is too often only formality – a performance for the routine of the service. In the modern pulpit, prayer is not the mighty force it was in Paul's life or Paul's ministry. Every preacher who does not make prayer a mighty factor in his own life and ministry is weak as a factor in God's work and powerless to project God's cause in this world.

Why sleep ye? rise and pray, lest ye enter into temptation (Luke 22:46).

Chapter 2

Depending Solely on God

Not that we are sufficient of ourselves to think anything as of ourselves, but our sufficiency is of God. – 2 Corinthians 3:5

But above all he [George Fox] excelled in prayer. The inwardness and weight of his spirit, the reverence and solemnity of his address and behavior, and the fewness and fullness of his words have often struck even strangers with admiration and reached others with consolation. The most amazing, living, reverend frame I ever felt or beheld, I must say, was his prayer. And truly it was a testimony that he knew and lived nearer to the Lord than other men, for they that know Him most will see most reason to approach Him with reverence and fear.
– William Penn on George Fox

Even a slight perversion can cause the sweetest graces to bear the bitterest fruit. *Know ye not that a little leaven leavens the whole lump? Purge out therefore the old leaven, that ye may be a new lump, as ye are unleavened* (1 Corinthians 5:6-7). The sun gives life, but sunstrokes bring death. Preaching is to give life; it may lock as well as unlock. Preaching is God's great institution for the planting and maturing of spiritual life. When properly executed, its benefits are untold; when wrongly executed, no evil can exceed its damaging results.

It is an easy matter to destroy the flock or ruin the pasture if the shepherd is not attentive; it is easy to capture the citadel or poison the food and water if the watchmen are asleep. As the preacher is invested with such gracious opportunities and exposed to so great evils involving many important responsibilities, it would be a parody on the shrewdness of the devil and defamation on his character and reputation if he did not bring his master influences to contaminate the preacher and the preaching. In light of this, Paul's exclamation, *Who is sufficient for these things?* is never out of order (2 Corinthians 2:16).

Paul says, *Our sufficiency is of God, who also has made us able ministers of the new testament, not of the letter, but of the Spirit: for the letter kills, but the Spirit gives life* (2 Corinthians 3:5-6). The true ministry is God-touched, God-enabled, and God-made. The Spirit of God anoints the preacher with power, and the fruit of the Spirit grows in his heart. The Spirit stimulates the man and empowers the Word, so his preaching gives life as the spring gives life. It gives life as the resurrection gives life; it gives vital life as the summer gives vital life, and it gives fruitful life as the autumn gives fruitful life.

The life-giving preacher is a man of God, whose heart is always thirsty for God, whose soul is always following God, and whose eye is only on God. By the power of God's Spirit, the flesh and the world have been crucified in this man, and his ministry is like the generous flood of a life-giving river. *For those that are of the Christ have crucified the flesh with its affections and lusts* (Galatians 5:24).

> The life-giving preacher is a man of God, whose heart is always thirsty for God, whose soul is always following God, and whose eye is only on God.

The preaching that kills is not spiritual preaching, for the ability of the preaching is not from God. Lower sources than God have given it energy and stimulant. The Spirit is not evident in the preacher or in his preaching. Many kinds of forces may be projected and stimulated by preaching that kills, but they are not spiritual forces. They may resemble spiritual forces, but they are only the shadow or the counterfeit. They may seem to have life, but the life is only an enticement.

The preaching that kills is still the letter – the dry, husky letter or the empty, bald shell. The letter may have the germ of life in it, but it has no breath of spring to revive it; they are winter seeds, as hard as the winter's soil and as icy as the winter's air, which do not thaw or germinate. This legalistic preaching has the truth, but even divine truth has no life-giving energy by itself; it must be energized by the Spirit with all God's forces at its back. *Now we are free from the law of death in which we were held, that we might serve in newness of Spirit, and not in the oldness of the letter* (Romans 7:6).

Truth that is not made alive by God's Spirit deadens as much as or more than error. It may be the pure truth, but without the Spirit, its shade and touch are deadly; its truth becomes error, and its light darkness. The letter-preaching is without anointing, neither mellowed nor oiled by the Spirit. There may be tears, but tears may only be summer's breath on a snow-covered iceberg, nothing but surface slush. Feelings and earnestness may be present, but they might be the emotion of the actor and the earnestness of the attorney.

From the kindling of his own sparks, the preacher may be eloquent over his own exegesis and earnest in delivering the product of his own brain. The professor may seize the moment and imitate the fire of the apostle; brains and nerves may serve the place and feign the work of God's Spirit, and by these forces the letter may glow and sparkle like an illuminated text, but this glow and sparkle will be as barren of life as the field sown with pearls.

The death-dealing element lies behind the words, the sermon, the occasion, the manner, and the actions. The great hindrance is in the preacher himself. He does not have the mighty, life-creating forces. There may be no discounting his orthodoxy, honesty, cleanness, or earnestness; but somehow the man, the inner man, in his secret places has never broken down and surrendered to God. His inner life is not a great highway for the transmission of God's message and God's power. Somehow, self, and not God, rules in the holy of holies, but *the Spirit is he that gives life; the flesh profits nothing* (John 6:63).

Somewhere, unconscious to the man, some spiritual nonconductor has touched his inner being, and the divine current has been arrested. His inner being has never felt its thorough spiritual bankruptcy, its utter powerlessness. He has never learned to cry out with an indescribable cry of self-despair and helplessness until God's power and God's fire come in and fill, purify, and empower. Self-esteem and self-ability in some pernicious shape have defamed and violated the temple, which should be held sacred for God. Life-giving preaching costs the preacher much – death to himself, crucifixion to the world, and agony of his own soul. Crucified preaching only can give life. Crucified preaching can come only from a crucified man.

I am crucified with Christ; nevertheless I live; yet not I, but Christ lives in me, and the life which I now live in the flesh I live by the faith of the Son of God, who loved me and gave himself for me. (Galatians 2:20)

Chapter 3

Preaching that Kills

Ye have made the commandment of God of no effect by your tradition. – Matthew 15:6

During this illness I was brought to examine my life in relation to eternity closer than I had done when in the enjoyment of health. In this examination relative to the performance of my duties towards my fellow creatures as a man, a Christian minister, and an officer of the church, I stood approved by my own conscience; but in relation to my Redeemer and Savior, the result was different. The coldness of my love to Him who first loved me and has done so much for me overwhelmed and confused me. I humbled myself, implored mercy, and renewed my covenant to strive to devote myself unreservedly to the Lord. – Bishop McKendree

The preaching that kills may be orthodox – dogmatically, firmly orthodox. We love orthodoxy. It is good. It is the best. It is clean, clear-cut teaching of

God's Word, the trophies won by truth in its conflict with error. Orthodoxy is the levee that faith has raised against the desolating floods of honest or reckless misbelief or unbelief; but orthodoxy, clear and hard as crystal, suspicious and militant, may only be the well-shaped, well-named, and well-learned letter – the letter that kills. Nothing is as dead as dead orthodoxy – too dead to speculate, too dead to think, study, or pray.

The preaching that kills may have insight and grasp of principles, and it may be scholarly and critical in taste. It may have every minutia of syntax and grammar in flawless construction. This preaching may trim the letter into its perfect pattern and illume it as Plato and Cicero can be illumined. The preacher may study it as a lawyer studies his textbooks to form his brief or to defend his case but still be cold and heartless. *Beware lest any man spoil you through philosophy and vain deceit, after the traditions of men, according to the elements of the world, and not after Christ* (Colossians 2:8).

Preaching the letter may be eloquent, enameled with poetry and rhetoric, sprinkled with prayer, spiced with sensation, and illumined by genius, but these are only the massive or chaste, costly mountings, the rare and beautiful flowers that drape the coffin of the corpse. The preaching which kills may be without scholarship, unmarked by any freshness of thought or feeling, clothed in tasteless generalities or lifeless specialties. It may be with careless, irregular style, savoring neither the prayer room nor the study, and not graced by thought, expression, or prayer. How wide and utter the desolation is under such preaching! How profound the spiritual death!

This preaching of the letter deals with the surface and shadow of things and not the things themselves. It does not penetrate the inner part. It has no deep insight into and no strong grasp of the hidden life of God's Word. It is true on the outside, but the outside is the hull that must be broken and penetrated for the kernel. The letter may be dressed to attract and be fashionable, but the attraction is not toward God, and it is not the fashion for heaven. That is why the apostle Paul wrote to the Corinthians that *I came . . . not with puffed up speech or wisdom to declare unto you the testimony of God. For I judged not to know anything among you, except Jesus Christ and him crucified* (1 Corinthians 2:1-2).

The failure is in the preacher. God has not made him. He has never been in the hands of God like clay in the hands of the potter. He has been busy writing the sermon, its theme, and the finish with examples and impressive force; but the deep things of God have not been sought, studied, fathomed, or experienced by him. He has never stood before *the Lord sitting upon a throne, high and lifted up* (Isaiah 6:1). He has never heard the seraphim song, never seen the vision, and never felt the rush of that overwhelming holiness. He has not cried out in weakness and guilt and had his life renewed, his heart touched, purged, and inflamed by the live coal from God's altar as Isaiah did. *Then one of the seraphim flew unto me, having a live coal in his hand which he had taken with the tongs from off the altar: And he laid it upon my mouth and said, Behold, this has touched thy lips; and it shall take away thy guilt, and thy sin shall be cleansed.* (Isaiah 6:6-7)

His ministry may draw people to him, to the church, to the form and ceremony, but no true drawings to God or sweet, holy, divine communion are induced. The church has been embellished but not edified, pleased but not sanctified. Life is suppressed; a chill is in the summer air; the soil is baked. The city of our God becomes the city of the dead; the church becomes a graveyard, not an embattled army. Praise and prayer are stifled; worship is dead. The preacher and the preaching have helped sin, not holiness; they have populated hell, not heaven.

Preaching that kills is prayerless preaching. Without prayer, the preacher creates death and not life. The preacher who is weak in prayer is weak in life-giving forces. The preacher who has retired prayer as a conspicuous and largely prevailing element in his own character has severed his preaching of its distinctive, life-giving power.

Professional praying will always exist, but professional praying pushes the preaching to its deadly work. Professional praying chills and kills both preaching and praying. Much of the lax devotion and lazy, irreverent attitudes in congregational praying originate with professional praying in the pulpit. Long, rambling, dry, and hollow are the prayers in many pulpits. Without anointing or heart, they fall like a killing frost on all the graces of worship. Death-dealing prayers they are. Every vestige of devotion has perished under their breath. The deader they are, the longer they grow. A plea for short praying, live praying, real heart praying, praying by the Holy Spirit – direct, specific, passionate, simple, and anointed – is in order for the pulpit. A school to teach preachers how to pray as God envisions praying would be more beneficial to true devotion, true worship, and true preaching than all theological schools.

Stop! Pause! Consider! Where are we? What are we doing? Preaching to kill? Praying to kill? We are praying to God! The great God, the Maker of all worlds, the Judge of all men. What reverence! What simplicity! What sincerity! What truth in the inward parts is demanded! How real we must be! How hearty! Prayer to God is the noblest exercise, the loftiest effort of man and the most real thing! *I exhort therefore, that, first of all, supplications, prayers, intercessions, and giving of thanks, be made for all men* (1 Timothy 2:1).

Shall we not discard forever accursed preaching that kills and prayer that kills, and do the real thing, the mightiest thing – prayerful praying and life-creating preaching – to bring the mightiest force to bear on heaven and earth and draw on God's exhaustless and open treasury for the need and beggary of man?

And my speech and my preaching was not with enticing words of human wisdom, but in demonstration of the Spirit and of power, that your faith should not be founded in the wisdom of men, but in the power of God. (1 Corinthians 2:4-5)

Chapter 4

Pastoral Tendencies to Be Avoided

If ye then are risen with Christ, seek those things which are above, where the Christ sits at the right hand of God. – Colossians 3:1

Let us often look at David Brainerd, a missionary in the woods of America, pouring out his very soul before God for the perishing heathen without whose salvation nothing could make him happy. Prayer – secret, fervent, believing prayer – lies at the root of all personal lives. He had a mild and winning temper and a heart given up to God in his prayer closet religion. These are the attainments, which more than all knowledge or all other gifts, will fit us to become the instruments of God in the great work of human redemption.
– Carey's Brotherhood, Serampore

There are two extreme tendencies in the ministry. The one is to shut oneself off from communication with the people. The monk and the hermit were illustrations of this; they shut themselves off from men to be with God more. They failed, of course. Our being with God is of use only as we disperse its priceless benefits to men. This generation, neither the preacher nor the people, is very intent on God. Our hankering is not that way. We shut ourselves into our studies, and we become students, bookworms, Bible worms, and sermon makers. We are noted for literature, thoughts, and sermons, but the people and God, where are they? Out of heart, out of mind. Preachers who are great thinkers and great students must be the greatest prayers, or they will be the greatest backsliders and heartless professionals. They will be rationalistic and less than the least of preachers in God's estimation.

The other tendency is to thoroughly popularize the ministry. The preacher is no longer God's man, but a man of affairs, a man of the people. Even though Paul said to *set your sight on things above, not on things on the earth*, this preacher doesn't pray, because his mission is to the people (Colossians 3:2). If he can move the people and create an interest in church work, he is satisfied. His personal relationship with God is no factor in his work. Prayer has little or no place in his plans. The disaster and ruin of such a ministry cannot be computed by earthly arithmetic. What the preacher is in prayer to God for himself and for his people, so is his power to provide good to men and so is his true fruitfulness, his true fidelity to God and man for time and eternity.

It is impossible for the preacher to keep his spirit in harmony with the divine nature of his high calling without much prayer. To think the preacher can keep himself trim and fit in his work of the ministry by his drive in duty and laborious fidelity is a serious mistake. Even writing and delivering sermons, incessant and taxing as an art, a duty, work, or pleasure, will captivate, harden, and alienate the heart if the preacher neglects prayer. The scientist loses God in nature. The preacher may lose God in his sermon.

> Prayer freshens the heart of the preaching.

Prayer freshens the heart of the preaching, keeps it in tune with God and in sympathy with the people, and lifts the ministry out of the chilly air of a profession. It produces routine and moves every wheel with the capability and power of a divine anointing. Mr. Spurgeon said:

> Of course the preacher is above all others distinguished as a man of prayer. He prays as an ordinary Christian, or he would be a hypocrite. He prays more than ordinary Christians, or he would be disqualified for the office he has undertaken. If you as ministers are not very prayerful, you are to be pitied. If you become lax in secret devotion, not only will you need to be pitied but your people also, and the day will come in which you shall be ashamed and confounded. All our libraries and studies are mere emptiness compared with our prayer closets. Our seasons of fasting and prayer have been high days indeed: never has heaven's gate stood

wider, never have our hearts been nearer the central Glory.

The praying that makes a prayerful ministry is not a little praying put in as we add flavoring to give a pleasant taste, but the praying must be in the body and must form the blood and bones. *Pray without ceasing* (1 Thessalonians 5:17), because prayer is no light duty that is put into a corner; it is no piecemeal performance carried out in the fragments of time that have been snatched from business and other engagements of life. Prayerfulness requires the best of our time – the heart of our time and strength. It is not the closet absorbed in the study or swallowed up in the activities of ministerial duties, but it is the closet first, the study and activities second, so that both study and activities are freshened and made efficient by the prayer closet.

Prayer that affects one's ministry must give the same tone to one's life. The praying that gives color and capability to character is not a hurried pastime, but it must enter as strongly into the heart and life as when Christ *had offered up prayers and supplications with strong crying and tears unto him that was able to save him from death, was heard because of his reverent fear* (Hebrews 5:7). Praying must draw the soul into an agony of desire as Paul's did when he said, *I say the truth in Christ, I do not lie, my conscience also bearing me witness in the Holy Spirit, that I have great sorrow and continual pain in my heart* (Romans 9:1-2). It must be a fire and force like the *effectual fervent prayer* of James. *The effectual fervent prayer of a righteous man availeth much* (James 5:16 KJV). Prayer must be of the quality that when put into the golden censer and burned before God, it makes mighty spiritual suffering and revolutions.

Prayer is not a little habit pinned on us while we were tied to our mother's apron strings. Neither is it a little quarter of a minute's grace said over an hour's dinner, but it is a most serious work of our most serious years. It engages more time and appetite than our longest dinings or richest feasts. The prayer that makes much of our preaching must be made much of. The character of our praying will determine the character of our preaching. Light praying will make light preaching. Prayer makes preaching strong, anoints it, and makes it stick. In every ministry producing much good, prayer has always been a serious business.

The preacher must be preeminently a man of prayer. His heart must graduate from the school of prayer where only the heart can learn to preach. No learning can make up for the failure to pray. No earnestness, no diligence, no study, no gifts will supply its lack.

Talking to men for God is a great thing, but talking to God for men is greater still. He will never talk well and with real success to men for God who has not learned how to talk well to God for men. More than this, prayerless words in the pulpit and out of it are deadening words.

> *As the branch cannot bear fruit of itself, except it abides in the vine, no more can ye, except ye abide in me. I AM the vine, ye are the branches:*

he that abides in me, and I in him, the same brings forth much fruit; for without me ye can do nothing. (John 15:4-5)

Chapter 5

The Preacher's Main Business is Prayer

And we will give ourselves continually to prayer and to the ministry of the word. – Acts 6:4

You know the value of prayer: it is precious beyond all price. Never, never neglect it.
– Sir Thomas Buxton

Prayer is the first thing, the second thing, the third thing necessary to a minister. Pray, then, my dear brother; pray, pray, pray.
– Edward Payson

Prayer, in the preacher's life, in the preacher's study, and in the preacher's pulpit must be a conspicuous and all-encompassing force and an eye-catching feature. It must play no secondary part or be a mere coating. The preacher is given the duty to be with his Lord all night in prayer. To train himself in self-denying prayer, he is charged to look to his Master who, *rising up a great while before day, he went out and departed into a solitary place and prayed there* (Mark 1:35). The preacher's study ought to be a closet, a Bethel, an altar, a vision, and a ladder, so that every thought might ascend heavenward before it goes manward, and every part of the sermon might carry the fragrance of heaven, because God was in the study.

As the engine never moves until the fire is kindled, so preaching, with all its machinery, perfection, and polish, is at a dead standstill, as far as spiritual results are concerned, until prayer has kindled and created the steam. The texture, fineness, and strength of the sermon are rubbish unless the mighty impulse of prayer is in it, through it, and behind it. The preacher must move God by prayer toward the people before he can move the people to God by his words. The preacher must have had audience and ready access to God before he can have access to the people. Let him *come boldly unto the throne of his grace, that* [he] *may obtain mercy and find grace to help in time of need* (Hebrews 4:16). An open way to God for the preacher is the surest pledge of an open way to the people.

> It is necessary to iterate and reiterate that prayer as a mere habit or performance rendered by routine or in a professional way is a dead and rotten thing.

It is necessary to iterate and reiterate that prayer as a mere habit or performance rendered by routine or in a professional way is a dead and rotten thing. Such praying has no connection with the praying for which we plead. We are stressing true praying that engages and sets on fire every high element of the preacher's being and is born in vital oneness with Christ and the fullness of the Holy Spirit. It springs from the deep, overflowing fountains of tender compassion and unending concern for man's eternal good, and depicts a thorough conviction of the preacher's difficult and delicate work and the imperative need of God's mightiest help. Praying grounded on these solemn and profound convictions is the only true praying. Preaching backed by such praying is the only preaching that sows the seeds of eternal life in human hearts and builds men up for heaven.

There may be popular preaching, pleasant preaching, and preaching of much intellectual, literary, and brainy force with its measure and form of good, with little or no praying. But the preaching that secures God's end must be born of prayer, delivered with the energy and spirit of prayer, followed, developed, and kept in vital force in the hearts of the hearers by preachers' prayers, long after the occasion has passed.

We may excuse the spiritual poverty of our preaching in many ways, but the true secret will be found in the lack of urgent prayer for God's presence in the power of the Holy Spirit. There are innumerable preachers who can deliver masterful sermons, but the effects are short-lived and do not enter as a factor into the regions of the spirit where the fearful war between God and Satan, heaven and hell, is being waged, because they are not made powerfully militant and spiritually victorious by prayer.

The preachers who gain mighty results for God are the men who have prevailed in their pleadings with God before venturing to plead with men. The preachers who are the mightiest in their closets with God are the mightiest in their pulpits with men. They understand the writer of James who said, *if any of you lacks wisdom, let them ask of God (who gives abundantly to all, and without reproach), and it shall be given them* (James 1:5).

Preachers are mere humans who are exposed to and often caught by the strong drifting of human progress. Praying is spiritual work, and human nature does not like taxing, spiritual work. Human nature wants to sail to heaven under a favoring breeze on a full, smooth sea. Prayer is humbling work. It disparages intellect and pride, crucifies vainglory, and signs our spiritual bankruptcy. All these are hard for flesh and blood to bear. It is easier not to pray than to bear this work. So we come to one of the crying evils of these times, maybe of all times – little or no praying. Of these two evils, perhaps little praying is worse than no praying. Little praying is a kind of make-believe, a salve for the conscience, a farce, and a delusion.

The little value we put on prayer is evident from the little time we give to it. The time given to prayer by the average preacher scarcely counts in the sum of the daily total. Frequently, the preacher's only praying is by his bedside at night as he is ready for bed and soon to be in it, and perhaps the addition of a few hasty snatches of prayer before he is dressed in the morning. How feeble, vain, and little is such praying compared to the time and energy devoted to praying by holy men in and out of the Bible. How poor and barren our petty, childish praying is compared to the habits of the true men of God in all ages!

God commits the keys of his kingdom to men who think praying is their main business and devote time to it according to this high estimate of its importance. *And the LORD said unto him, I have heard thy prayer and thy supplication that thou hast made in my presence. I have sanctified this house, which thou hast built, to put my name there for ever, and my eyes and my heart shall be there all the days.* (1 Kings 9:3). By them, he works his spiritual wonders in this world. Great praying is the sign and seal of God's great leaders and the earnest of the conquering forces with which God will crown their labors.

The preacher is commissioned to pray as well as to preach. His mission is incomplete if he does not do both well. The preacher may speak with all the eloquence of men and of angels, but unless he can pray with a faith that draws all heaven to his aid, his preaching will be *as sounding brass or a tinkling cymbal* for permanent God-honoring, soul-saving uses (1 Corinthians 13:1).

Chapter 6

What Prayer Can Do for Your Ministry

Rejoicing in hope, patient in tribulation, constant in prayer. – Romans 12:12

The principal cause of my leanness and unfruitfulness is due to an unaccountable backwardness to pray. I can write or read or converse or hear with a ready heart, but prayer is more spiritual and inward than any of these, and the more spiritual any duty is, the more my carnal heart is apt to stay away from it. Prayer and patience and faith are never disappointed. I have long since learned that if ever I was to be a minister, faith and prayer must make me one. When I can find my heart in frame and liberty for prayer, everything else is comparatively easy.
– Richard Newton

It may be declared a spiritual axiom that in every successful ministry, prayer is an evident and controlling force – evident and controlling in the life of the preacher and evident and controlling in the deep spirituality of his work. As Paul prayed:

For this cause I bow my knees unto the Father of our Lord Jesus Christ (of whom the whole family in the heavens and on earth is named), that he would grant you, according to the riches of his glory, to be strengthened with might by his Spirit in the inner man, that the Christ may dwell in your hearts by faith, that ye, being rooted and grounded in charity, may be able to well comprehend with all saints what is the breadth and length and depth and height and to know the charity of the Christ (Ephesians 3:14-19).

A ministry may be a thoughtful ministry without prayer, and the preacher may secure fame and popularity without prayer. The whole machinery of the preacher's life and work may be run without the oil of prayer or with scarcely enough to grease one cog, but no ministry can be a spiritual one that secures holiness in the preacher and in his people without prayer being made an evident and controlling force.

The preacher that prays indeed puts God into the work. God does not come into the preacher's work as a matter of course or on general principles, but he comes by prayer and special urgency. That we will find God in the day that we seek him with the whole heart is as true of the preacher as of the penitent. *Then ye shall call upon me, and ye shall walk in my ways and pray unto me, and I will hearken unto you. And ye shall seek me, and find me, for ye shall seek me with all your heart*

(Jeremiah 29:12-13). A prayerful ministry is the only ministry that brings the preacher into sympathy with the people. Prayer essentially unites people, as it unites people to the divine.

A prayerful ministry is the only ministry qualified for the high offices and responsibilities of the preacher. Colleges, learning, books, theology, and preaching cannot make a preacher, but praying does. The apostles' commission to preach was a blank, until it was filled in by the Pentecost that praying brought. *They returned unto Jerusalem from the mount called Olivet... These all continued with one accord in prayer and supplication ... And when the day of Pentecost was fully come, they were all with one accord in one place. And they were all filled with the Holy Spirit* (Acts 1:12, 14; 2:1, 4).

A prayerful minister has passed beyond the regions of the popular, beyond the man of mere affairs, worldly matters, and pulpit attractiveness. He has passed beyond the ecclesiastical organization and into a loftier and mightier region, the region of the spiritual. Holiness is the product of his work; transformed hearts and lives proclaim the reality of his work – its true and substantial nature. God is with him. His ministry is not projected on worldly or surface principles. He has accumulated and been schooled in the things of God. His long, deep communion with God about his people and the agony of his wrestling spirit have crowned him as a prince in the things of God. The iciness of the mere professional has long since melted under the intensity of his praying.

The superficial results of many a ministry and the deadness of others are to be found in the lack of praying. No ministry can succeed without much praying, and this praying must be fundamental, ever abiding, and ever increasing. The text and the sermon should be the result of prayer. The study should be bathed in prayer, all its duties saturated with prayer, and its whole spirit the spirit of prayer. "I am sorry that I have prayed so little," was the deathbed regret of one of God's chosen ones, a sad and remorseful regret for a preacher. "I want a life of greater, deeper, truer prayer," said the late Archbishop Tait. We may all say this, and we may all secure it.

God's true preachers have been distinguished by one great feature: they were men of prayer. Differing often in many things, they have always had a common center. They have started from different points and traveled by different roads, but they converged to one point: they were one in prayer. To them God was the center of attraction, and prayer was the path that led to God. These men prayed – not occasionally and not a little at regular or at odd times. They prayed so that their prayers entered into and shaped their characters; they prayed to affect their own lives and the lives of others; they prayed to make the history of the church and influence the events of the times. They spent much time in prayer, not because they marked the shadow on the dial or the hands on the clock, but because it was so momentous and engaging a business to them that they could scarcely quit.

To them prayer was what it was to Paul – a striving with earnest effort of soul; it was that to Jacob – a wrestling and prevailing. And to Christ it was a *strong crying and tears* (Hebrews 5:7). They prayed *always with all prayer and supplication in the Spirit and watching in this with all perseverance* (Ephesians 6:18). The *effectual fervent prayer* has been the mightiest weapon of God's mightiest soldiers.

The statement in the book of James about Elijah says that he *was a man subject to passions like unto ours, and he asked in prayer that it might not rain, and it did not rain on the earth for three years and six months. And he prayed again, and the heaven gave rain, and the earth brought forth her fruit* (James 5:17-18). This statement is a picture of all prophets and preachers who have moved their generation for God, and it shows by whom they worked their wonders.

Chapter 7

Make Time for Prayer

Evening and morning and at noon I will pray and cry aloud, and he shall hear my voice.
– Psalm 55:17

The great masters and teachers in Christian doctrine have always found in prayer their highest source of illumination. Not to go beyond the limits of the English Church, it is recorded of Bishop Andrews that he spent five hours daily on his knees. The greatest practical resolves that have enriched and beautified human life in Christian times have been arrived at in prayer.
– Canon Liddon

Public prayers, as a rule, ought to be short and condensed, but in our private communion with God, time is an essential, valuable feature. Much time spent with God is the secret of all successful praying. Prayer that is felt as a mighty force is the immediate product of much time spent with God. Our short prayers owe their point and efficiency to the long ones that have preceded them. The short, prevailing prayer cannot be prayed by one who has not prevailed with God in a mightier struggle of long endurance.

Jacob's victory of faith could not have been gained without that all-night wrestling. God's acquaintance is not made by pop calls. God does not bestow his gifts on the casual or hasty comers and goers. Much time with God alone is the secret of knowing him and of influence with him, for *the LORD is near unto all those that call upon him, to all that call upon him in truth* (Psalm 145:18). He yields to the persistency of a faith that knows him. He bestows his richest gifts upon those who declare their desire for and appreciation of those gifts by the constancy as well as the earnestness of their solicitations. Christ, who is our example in this, spent many whole nights in prayer. His custom was to pray much. He had his habitual place to pray. Many long seasons of praying make up his history and character. Paul prayed day and night. It took time from very important interests for Daniel to pray three times a day. David's morning-noon-and-night praying was doubtless very lengthy on many occasions. While we have no specific account of the time these Bible saints spent in prayer, the indications are that they consumed much time in prayer, and on some occasions long seasons of praying was their custom.

We do not want anyone to think that the value of their prayers is to be measured by the clock, but our purpose is to impress on our minds the necessity of being alone with God for a significant amount of time. If this has not been produced by our faith, then our faith is of a feeble and shallow type, but as Paul told the Colossians: *persevere in prayer and watch in the same with thanksgiving, praying also together for us that God would open unto us the door of the word.* (Colossians 4:2-3)

The men who have illustrated Christ most fully in their character and have affected the world most powerfully for him have been men who spent so much time with God as to make it a dominant occurrence in their lives. Charles Simeon devoted the hours from four until eight in the morning to God.

Mr. Wesley spent two hours in prayer every day. He began at four in the morning. Someone who knew him well wrote, "He thought prayer to be more his business than anything else, and I have seen him come out of his closet with a serenity of face next to shining."

John Fletcher stained the walls of his room with the breath of his prayers. Sometimes he would pray all night – always, frequently, and with great earnestness. His whole life was a life of prayer. "I would not rise from my seat," he said, "without lifting my heart to God." His greeting to a friend was always, "Do I meet you praying?"

Luther said, "If I fail to spend two hours in prayer each morning, the devil gets the victory through the day. I have so much business I cannot get on without spending three hours daily in prayer." He had a motto: "He that has prayed well has studied well."

Archbishop Leighton was alone with God so much

that he seemed to be in perpetual meditation. "Prayer and praise were his business and his pleasure," says his biographer.

Bishop Ken was with God so much that his soul was said to be God enamored. He was with God before the clock struck three every morning.

Bishop Asbury said, "I propose to rise at four o'clock as often as I can and spend two hours in prayer and meditation." Samuel Rutherford, the fragrance of whose devotion is still rich, rose at three in the morning to meet God in prayer, as the psalmist said, *My voice shalt thou hear in the morning, O LORD; early will I present myself unto thee and wait* (Psalm 5:3).

Joseph Alleine rose at four o'clock for his business of praying until eight. If he heard other tradesmen working at their business before he was up, he would exclaim, "Oh, how this shames me! Doth not my Master deserve more than theirs?" He who has learned this trade well draws at will, and with acceptance of heaven's unfailing reserves.

One of the holiest and among the most gifted of Scotch preachers said, "I ought to spend the best hours in communion with God. It is my noblest and most fruitful employment and is not to be thrust into a corner. The morning hours from six to eight are the most uninterrupted and should be thus employed. After tea is my best hour, and that should be solemnly dedicated to God. I should not give up the good old habit of prayer before going to bed; I also need to guard against sleep. When I awake in the night, I should rise and pray. A little time after breakfast might be given to intercession." This was the praying plan of Robert McCheyne. The memorable Methodist band of men shame us with their praying. "From four to five in the morning, private prayer; from five to six in the evening, private prayer."

John Welch, the holy and wonderful Scotch preacher, thought the day ill-spent if he did not spend eight or ten hours in prayer. He kept a plaid blanket that he might wrap himself in when he arose to pray at night. His wife would complain when she found him lying on the ground weeping. He would reply, "Oh, woman, I have the souls of three thousand to answer for, and I know not how it is with many of them!"

I exhort therefore, that, first of all, supplications, prayers, intercessions, and giving of thanks, be made for all men, for kings, and for all that are in authority that we may lead a quiet and peaceable life in all godliness and integrity.
(1 Timothy 2:1-2)

Chapter 8

Examples of Praying Men

I desire, therefore, that the men in every place, pray, lifting up holy hands, without wrath and strife. – 1 Timothy 2:8

The act of praying is the very highest energy of which the human mind is capable; praying, that is, with the total concentration of the faculties. The great mass of worldly men and of learned men are absolutely incapable of prayer.
– Coleridge

Bishop Wilson said, "In Henry Martyn's journals, the spirit of prayer, the time he devoted to the duty, and his fervor in it are the first things which strike me."

Edward Payson wore the hardwood boards into grooves where his knees pressed so often and so long. His biographer relates, "His continuing instant in prayer, whatever his circumstances, is the most noticeable fact in his history and points out the duty of all who would rival his greatness. . . . His distinguished and almost uninterrupted success to a great measure can be ascribed to his ardent and persevering prayers."

Christ was most precious to the Marquis DeRenty who ordered his servant to call him from his devotions at the end of half an hour. The servant at the time saw his face through a crack, and it was marked with such holiness that he hated to disturb him. His lips were moving, but he was perfectly silent. He waited until three hours had passed, then he called to him. When he arose from his knees, he said that the half hour was very short when he was communing with Christ.

David Brainerd said, "I love to be alone in my cottage, where I can spend much time in prayer."

William Bramwell is famous in Methodist history for personal holiness, his wonderful success in preaching, and the marvelous answers to his prayers. For hours at a time, he would pray. He almost lived on his knees. He went over his circuits like a flame of fire. The fire was kindled by the time he spent in prayer. He often spent as much as four hours of prayer at a time.

Bishop Lancelot Andrewes spent the greatest part of five hours every day in prayer and devotion.

When the ark of the covenant had been brought to Jerusalem, King David told the Israelites to *seek the LORD and his strength, seek his face continually* (1 Chronicles 16:11).

Sir Henry Havelock always spent the first two hours of each day alone with God. If the residence stirred at 6:00 a.m., he would rise at 4:00 a.m. He took to heart the words of the psalmist: *But unto thee have I cried, O*

LORD; and in the morning shall my prayer come before thee (Psalm 88:13).

Earl Cairns rose daily at six o'clock to secure an hour and a half for the study of the Bible and for prayer, before conducting family worship at a quarter to eight.

Dr. Judson's success in prayer is attributed to the fact that he gave much time to prayer. On this point, he said:

> Arrange your days, if possible, so that you can leisurely devote two or three hours every day or so merely to devotional exercises – to the very act of secret prayer and communion with God. Endeavor seven times a day to withdraw from business and company and lift up your soul to God in solitude. Begin the day by rising after midnight and devoting some time in the silence and darkness of the night to this sacred work. Let the hour of dawn find you at the same work. Let the hours of nine, twelve, three, six, and nine at night also find you in prayer. Be resolute in this cause. Make all practical sacrifices to maintain this schedule. Consider that your time is short, and business and company must not be allowed to rob you of your God.

Do we consider these impossible, fanatical directions? Dr. Judson impressed an empire for Christ and laid the foundation for God's kingdom with imperishable rock in the heart of Burma. He was successful as one of the few men who mightily impressed the world for Christ. Many men with greater gifts and genius and learning have made no such impression; their religious work is like footsteps in the sands, but Dr. Judson has engraved his work on the hardened hearts. The secret of its profoundness and endurance is found in the fact that he gave time to prayer. He kept the iron red-hot with prayer, and God's skill fashioned it with enduring power. No man can do a great and enduring work for God who is not a man of prayer, and no man can be a man of prayer who does not give much time to praying.

> No man can be a man of prayer who does not give much time to praying.

Is it true that prayer is simply the compliance with habit – dull and mechanical? A petty performance into which we are trained until tameness, shortness, and superficiality are its chief components? *But when ye pray, use not vain repetitions as the worldly do* (Matthew 6:7a).

"Is it true that prayer is little more than the half-passive play of sentiment that flows sluggishly through the minutes or hours of easy meditation?" Canon Liddon continues:

> Let those who have really prayed give the answer. They sometimes describe prayer with the patriarch Jacob as a wrestling together with an Unseen Power, which may last late into the night hours or even to the break of day.

Sometimes they refer to common intercession with the apostle Paul as a concerted struggle. When praying, they have their eyes fixed on the Great Intercessor in Gethsemane and upon the drops of blood that fall to the ground in the agony of resignation and sacrifice.

Persistence is of the essence of successful prayer; it is not dreaminess but sustained work. It is through prayer especially that the kingdom of heaven suffers violence and the violent take it by force. It was a saying of Bishop Hamilton that 'No man is likely to do much good in prayer if he does not look upon it as preparation for a work and persevere with all the earnestness which we bring to other subjects that are most interesting and necessary to us.'

> *I arose before the dawning of the morning and cried: I waited in thy word. My eyes anticipate the night watches that I might meditate in thy spoken word. Hear my voice according to thy mercy; O LORD, cause me to live according to thy judgment.* (Psalm 119:147-149)

Chapter 9

Early Morning Prayer

Cause me to hear thy mercy in the morning, for in thee do I trust; cause me to know the way in which I should walk, for I lift up my soul unto thee. – Psalm 143:8

I ought to pray before seeing anyone. Often when I sleep long, or meet with others early, it is eleven or twelve o'clock before I begin secret prayer. This is a wretched system. It is unscriptural. Christ arose before day and went into a solitary place. David says, "Early will I seek thee"; "Thou shalt early hear my voice." Family prayer loses much of its power and sweetness, and I can do no good to those who come to seek from me. The conscience feels guilty, the soul unfed, the lamp untrimmed. Then when in secret prayer the soul is often out of tune. I feel it is far better to begin with God – to see His face first, to get my soul near him before it is near another. – Robert Murray McCheyne

The men who have done the most for God in this world have been on their knees early in the day.

He who fritters away the early morning, its opportunity, and its freshness in other pursuits than seeking God will make poor headway seeking him the rest of the day. *By much slothfulness the building decays, and through idleness of the hands the rain drips throughout the house* (Ecclesiastes 10:18). If God is not first in our thoughts and efforts in the morning, he will be in the last place for the remainder of the day.

Behind this early rising and early praying is the vibrant desire that presses us into this pursuit after God. Morning listlessness is the sign of a listless heart. The heart that is slow in seeking God in the morning has lost its relish for God. David's heart was passionate for God. He hungered and thirsted after God, so he sought God early – before daylight. He proclaimed, *I stretched forth my hands unto thee; my soul thirsted after thee, as a thirsty land* (Psalm 143:6).

> If God is not first in our thoughts and efforts in the morning, he will be in the last place for the remainder of the day.

The bed and sleep could not chain his soul in its eagerness for God. Christ longed for communion with God; so, rising a great while before day, he would go out to the mountain to pray. When the disciples were fully awake, they were ashamed of their indulgence in sleep, but they knew where to find him. We could consider the list of men who have impressed the world for God, and we would find them pursuing God early in the morning.

A desire for God that cannot break the chains of sleep is a weak thing and will do little good for God after it has indulged itself fully. The desire for God that keeps so far behind the devil and the world at the beginning of the day will never catch up.

Simply the getting up is not what puts men to the front and makes them generals in God's hosts, but it is the passionate desire that stirs and breaks all self-indulgent chains. But the getting up gives expression, increase, and strength to the desire. If they had lain in bed and indulged themselves, the desire would have been quenched. The desire aroused them and put them on the road for God. This heeding and acting on the call gave their faith its grasp on God and gave their hearts the sweetest and fullest revelation of God. This strength of faith and fullness of revelation made them saints by reputation, and the aura of their sainthood has come down to us, so that we have entered into the enjoyment of their conquests. But we take our fill in enjoyment and not in productions. We build their tombs and write their epitaphs but are careful not to follow their examples.

We need a generation of preachers who seek God and seek him early, as Solomon said of God, *I love those that love me, and those that seek me early shall find me* (Proverbs 8:17). We need preachers who give the freshness and dew of effort to God and secure in return the freshness and fullness of his power that he may be as the dew to them, full of gladness and strength through all the heat and labor of the day. Our laziness after God is our crying sin. The children of this world are far wiser than we are. They are busy at work early and late. We do not seek God with passion and diligence. No man experiences God who does not follow after him intently, and no soul follows intently after God who is not seeking him in the early morning.

> *I will go and return to my place until they acknowledge their guilt and seek my face; in their affliction they will seek me early.* (Hosea 5:15)

Chapter 10

Devoted Prayer

The LORD is good unto those that wait in him, to the soul that seeks him. It is good to wait quietly in the salvation of the LORD.
– Lamentations 3:25-26

There is a manifest want of spiritual influence on the minister of the present day. I feel it in my own case and I see it in that of others. . . . We are laying ourselves out more than is expedient to meet one man's taste and another man's prejudices. The ministry is a grand and holy affair, and it should find in us a simple habit and a holy but humble indifference to all consequences. The leading defect in Christian ministers is want of a devotional habit. – Richard Cecil

Never was there a greater need for saintly men and women, but more crucial is the call for saintly, God-devoted preachers. The world moves with gigantic strides, and *in time past ye walked according to the course of this world, according to the will of the prince of the power of this air, the spirit that now works in the sons of disobedience* (Ephesians 2:2). Satan has his hold and rule on the world, and he labors to make all its movements further his ends.

Religion must do its best work and present its most attractive and perfect models. By every means, modern sainthood must be inspired by the grandest ideals and greatest possibilities through the Spirit. Paul lived on his knees, so that the Ephesian church might measure the heights, breadths, and depths of an unmeasurable saintliness. He prayed that they might *be able to well comprehend with all saints what is the breadth and length and depth and height and to know the charity of the Christ, which passes all knowledge, that ye might be filled with all the fullness of God* (Ephesians 3:18-19).

Epaphras laid himself out with the exhaustive toil and strenuous conflict of fervent prayer for the Colossian church. Paul related to them that Epaphras was *always labouring fervently for you in prayers, that ye may stand firm, perfect and fulfilled in all the will of God* (Colossians 4:12). Everywhere, everything in apostolic times was on the pathway that the people of God might each and *all come forth in the unity of the faith and of the knowledge of the Son of God unto a perfect man, unto the measure of the coming of age of the Christ* (Ephesians 4:13).

No premium was given to dwarfs, no encouragement to an old baby. The babies were to grow and mature; the old were to bear fruit in their old age and be fat and flourishing instead of weak and insecure. The most sacred thing in religion is holy men and holy women. No amount of money, genius, or culture can move things for God. Holiness energizing the soul, the whole man aflame with love, and the desire for more faith, more prayer, more zeal, and more consecration is the secret of power. We need these and must have them; men must be the incarnation of this God-inflamed devotedness.

God's purpose has been delayed, his cause crippled, and his name dishonored for the lack of holy men and women. The loftiest and most-gifted genius, the most-learned and refined education, position, dignity, honored titles, or high clerical rank cannot move this chariot of our God. It is a fiery one, and only fiery forces can move it. The genius of a Milton fails, and the imperial strength of a Leo fails.

> No amount of money, genius, or culture can move things for God.

But David Brainerd's spirit could move it. Brainerd's spirit was on fire for God and on fire for souls. Nothing earthly, worldly, or selfish came in to diminish in the least the intensity of this all-impelling and all-consuming force and flame.

Prayer is the creator as well as the channel of devotion. The spirit of devotion is the spirit of prayer. Prayer and devotion are united as soul and body are united, as life and the heart are united. There is no real prayer without devotion, no devotion without prayer. The preacher must be surrendered to God in the holiest devotion. He is not a professional man; his ministry is not a profession. It is a divine institution, a divine devotion. He is devoted to God. His aim and ambition are for God and to God, and to such as these, prayer is as essential as food is to life.

Above everything else, the preacher must be devoted to God. The preacher's relationship to God is the insignia and credentials of his ministry. These must be clear, conclusive, and unmistakable. No common, surface type of devotion can be his. If he does not excel in grace, he does not excel at all. If he does not preach by life, character, and conduct, he does not preach at all. A preacher must, as Paul taught Timothy, be *an example of the faithful in word, in conversation, in charity, in spirit, in faith, in purity.* (1 Timothy 3:4-7).

If his devotion is light, his preaching may be as soft and as sweet as music and as gifted as Apollo, but its weight will be a feather's weight – visionary and fleeting as the morning cloud or the early dew. There is no substitute for devotion to God in the preacher's character and conduct.

Devotions to a church, to opinions, to an organization, or to orthodoxy are paltry, misleading, and vain when they become the source of inspiration; they become hostile to the call. God must be the mainspring of the preacher's effort, the fountain and crown of all his toil. The name and honor of Jesus Christ and the advancement of his cause must be his all. The preacher must have no inspiration except the name of Jesus Christ, no ambition besides Christ glorified, and no toil but for him. Then prayer will be a source of his illumination, the means of perpetual motivation, and the gauge of his success. The perpetual aim, the only ambition, that the preacher can cherish, is to have God with him.

Never did the cause of God need perfect illustrations of the possibilities of prayer more than in this age. No age and no person can be examples of the gospel power except the ages or persons of deep and earnest prayer. A prayerless age will have few examples of divine power. Prayerless hearts will never rise to Alpine heights. This generation may be a better age than the past, but there is an infinite distance between the betterment of an age by the force of an advancing civilization, and its betterment by the increase of holiness and Christlikeness by the energy of prayer.

The Jews were much better when Christ came than in the ages before. It was the golden age of their pharisaical religion. Their golden religious age crucified Christ. There had never been more praying, never less praying, never more sacrifices, never less sacrifice, never more idolatry, never less idolatry. They had never experienced more temple worship but less of God worship, never more lip service but never less heart service. God was worshiped by lips whose hearts and hands crucified God's Son! There were never more churchgoers but never fewer saints. Because of this, Jesus said to the scribes and Pharisees:

Ye hypocrites, well did Isaiah prophesy of you, saying, This people draws nigh unto me with their mouth and honours me with their lips, but their heart is far from me. But in vain do they worship me, teaching doctrines and commandments of men. (Matthew 15:7-9)

It is prayer force that makes saints. Holy characters are formed by the power of real praying. The more true saints, the more praying; the more praying, the more true saints.

O God, thou art my God; early will I seek thee; my soul thirsts for thee; my flesh longs for thee in a dry and thirsty land where there is no water; in this manner I beheld thee in holiness when I beheld thy power and thy glory. Because thy mercy is better than life, my lips shall praise thee. Thus will I bless thee in my life; in thy name shall I lift up my hands. (Psalm 63:1-4)

Chapter 11

An Example of Devotion

Draw near to God, and he will draw near to you. Cleanse your hands, ye sinners; and purify your hearts, ye double minded. – James 4:8

I urge upon you communion with Christ, a growing communion. There are curtains to be drawn aside in Christ that we never saw, and new foldings of love in him. . . . Therefore dig deep and sweat and labor and take pains for him, and set by as much time in the day for him as you can. He will be won in the labor.
– Samuel Rutherford

God has now, and has had before, many devoted, prayerful preachers – men with lives in which prayer has been a mighty, controlling, conspicuous force. The world has felt their power, and God has felt and honored that power. His cause has moved mightily and swiftly by their prayers; their characters have beamed holiness with a divine radiance.

God found one of the men he was looking for in

David Brainerd, whose work and name have gone into history. He was no ordinary man but was capable of shining in any company. As the peer of the wise and gifted ones, he was eminently suited to fill the most attractive pulpits and labor among the most refined and the cultured who were anxious to secure him for their pastor.

Jonathan Edwards, president of Princeton, bears testimony that he was "a young man of distinguished talents, had extraordinary knowledge of men and things, had rare conversational powers, excelled in his knowledge of theology, and was truly an extraordinary saint, especially in all matters relating to experiencing religion for one so young. I never knew his equal of his age and standing for clear and accurate notions of the nature and essence of true religion. His manner in prayer was almost incomparable, such as I have rarely known an equal. His learning was very considerable, and he had extraordinary gifts for the pulpit."

No holier story has been recorded in recent centuries than that of David Brainerd; no miracle attests with more godly force the truth of Christianity than the life and work of such a man. Alone in the savage wilds of America, he struggled day and night with a mortal disease. He was not schooled in the care of souls and only had access to the Indians through the bungling medium of a pagan interpreter for a large portion of time. With the Word of God in his heart and in his hand, his soul fired with the divine flame, and a place and time to pour out his soul to God in prayer, he established the worship of God and secured all its gracious results.

The Indians were affected with a great change from the lowest conditions of an ignorant and debased heathenism to pure, devout, and intelligent Christians; they were *transformed by the renewing of* [their] *soul that* [they] *may experience what is that good and well pleasing and perfect will of God* (Romans 12:2). With all vices reformed, the external duties of Christianity were at once embraced and acted on. Family prayer was set up, and the Sabbath was instituted and religiously observed. The internal graces of religion were exhibited with growing sweetness and strength.

The cause of these results is found in David Brainerd himself, not in the conditions or accidents but in the man Brainerd. He was God's man, for he put God first and last and all the time. God could flow unhindered through him. The omnipotence of grace was neither restrained nor hindered by the conditions of his heart. The whole channel was broad and clean for God's fullest and most powerful passage, so that God could come down with all his mighty forces on the hopeless, savage wilderness, and transform it into his blooming and fruitful garden. As Paul told Timothy, *be strong in the grace that is in Christ Jesus. And the things that thou has heard of me among many witnesses, the same commit thou to faithful men, who shall be able to teach others also* (2 Timothy 2:1-2). Nothing is too hard for God if he has the right kind of a man to do it.

Brainerd lived the life of holiness and prayer. His diary is full and monotonous with the record of his seasons of fasting, meditation, and rest. The time he spent in private prayer amounted to many hours daily. "When I return home," he said, "and give myself to meditation, prayer, and fasting, my soul longs for mortification, self-denial, humility, and divorcement from all things of the world."

"I have nothing to do," he said, "with earth, but only to labor in it honestly for God. I do not desire to live one minute for anything that earth can afford." He may have prayed with the psalmist: *Hear my prayer, O LORD, and give ear unto my cry; hold not thy peace at my tears: for I am a stranger with thee and a sojourner, as all my fathers were* (Psalm 39:12). After this high order, he prayed:

> Feeling somewhat of the sweetness of communion with God, the constraining force of his love, and how admirably it captivates the soul and makes all the desires and affections to center in God, I set this day apart for secret fasting and prayer. I entreat God to direct and bless me with regard to the great work that I have in view of preaching the gospel. May the Lord return to me and show me the light of his countenance.
>
> I had little life and power in the morning. Near the middle of the afternoon God enabled me to wrestle passionately in intercession for my absent friends, but at night the Lord visited me marvelously in prayer. I think my soul was never in such agony before. I felt no restraint,

AN EXAMPLE OF DEVOTION

> for the treasures of divine grace were opened to me. I wrestled for absent friends, for the ingathering of souls, for multitudes of poor souls, and for many that I thought were the children of God in many distant places. I was in such agony from noon sun until near dark that I was wet all over with sweat, but it seemed to me I had done nothing.
>
> Oh, my dear Saviour sweat blood for poor souls! I longed for more compassion toward them. I felt still in a sweet frame under a sense of divine love and grace, and I went to bed in that condition with my heart set on God.

It was prayer that gave his life and ministry their marvelous power.

The men of mighty prayer are men of spiritual might. Prayers never die. Brainerd's whole life was a life of prayer. *Yet the LORD will command his mercy in the daytime, and in the night his song shall be with me, and my prayer unto the God of my life* (Psalm 42:8). By day and by night, he prayed. Before preaching and after preaching, he prayed. Riding through the interminable solitudes of the forest, he prayed. On his bed of straw, he prayed. Retiring to the dense and lonely forests, he prayed. Hour by hour, day after day, early morning and late at night, he prayed and fasted; he poured out his soul, interceded, and communed with God.

He was with God mightily in prayer, and God was with him mightily. Because of that, though he is dead, yet he speaks and works and will speak and work until the end comes. Among the glorious ones of that glorious day, he will be with the first. Jonathan Edwards said of him:

> His life shows the right way to success in the works of the ministry. He sought it as the soldier seeks victory in a siege or battle or as a man who runs a race for a great prize. Animated with love for Christ and souls, how did he labor? Always fervently. Not only in word and doctrine, in public and in private, but in prayers by day and night, wrestling with God in secret and laboring in birth with unutterable groans and agonies until Christ was formed in the hearts of the people to whom he was sent. Like a true son of Jacob, he persevered in wrestling through all the darkness of the night, until the breaking of the day!

And Jacob was left alone, and a man wrestled with him until the breaking of the day.
(Genesis 32:24)

Chapter 12

Preparation of the Heart

If thou wilt receive my words and hide my commandments within thee so that thou incline thine ear unto wisdom and apply thine heart to intelligence, yea, if thou criest for understanding and givest thy voice unto intelligence, if thou seekest her as silver and searchest for her as for hid treasures, then shalt thou understand the fear of the LORD and find the knowledge of God. – Proverbs 2:1-5

For nothing reaches the heart but what is from the heart, or pierces the conscience but what comes from a living conscience. – William Penn

A sermon that has more head infused into it than heart will not come home with effectiveness to the hearers. – Robert Cecil

Prayer, with its numerous and many-sided forces, helps the mouth to utter the truth in its fullness and freedom. *My mouth shall speak wisdom; and the meditation of my heart intelligence* (Psalm 49:3). The preacher is to be prayed for; the preacher is made by prayer. The preacher's mouth is to be prayed for; his mouth is to be opened and filled by prayer. *For my mouth shall speak truth, and wickedness is an abomination to my lips. All the words of my mouth are in righteousness; there is nothing perverse or twisted in them* (Proverbs 8:7-8).

A holy mouth is made by much praying, and a brave mouth is made by much praying. The church and the world, God and heaven, owe much to Paul's mouth; Paul's mouth owed its power to prayer, as he said, *For we can do nothing against the truth, but for the truth. By which we are glad that we are weak and ye are strong, and even so we pray for your perfection* (2 Corinthians 13:8-9).

Praying makes the preacher a heart preacher.

How diverse, enduring, valuable, and helpful prayer is to the preacher in so many ways and at so many points in every way! One great value is that it helps his heart. Praying makes the preacher a heart preacher. Prayer puts the preacher's heart into the preacher's sermon; prayer puts the preacher's sermon into the preacher's heart.

The heart makes the preacher. Men of great hearts are great preachers. Men of bad hearts may do a measure of good, but this is rare. The hireling and the stranger may help the sheep at some points, but the good shepherd with the good shepherd's heart is the one who will bless the sheep and answer the full measure of the shepherd's place.

We have emphasized sermon preparation until we

have lost sight of the important thing to be prepared – the heart. A prepared heart is much better than a prepared sermon. A prepared heart will make a prepared sermon.

Volumes have been written to demonstrate the mechanics and proficiency of developing a sermon, until we have become possessed with the idea that this scaffolding is the building. The young preacher has been taught to apply all his strength on the form, creativity, and beauty of his sermon as a mechanical and intellectual product. We have thereby cultivated a fierce appetite among the people and raised the clamor for talent instead of grace, eloquence instead of devotion, rhetoric instead of revelation, reputation and brilliance instead of holiness. By this method, we have lost the true idea of preaching and preaching power. We have no pungent conviction of sin; we have lost the rich experience and elevated Christian character and the authority over consciences and lives, which always results from genuine preaching.

It would not do to say that preachers study too much. Some of them do not study at all; others do not study enough. Many do not study the right way to show themselves workmen approved of God, as Paul instructed Timothy: *Study to show thyself approved unto God, a workman that has nothing to be ashamed of, rightly dividing the word of truth* (2 Timothy 2:15). But our great lack is not in our heads but in our hearts; not lack of knowledge but lack of holiness is our sad and telling defect. It is not that we know too much, but that we do not meditate on God and his Word and watch and fast and pray enough. The heart is the great hindrance to our preaching. Words full of divine truth find nonconductors in our hearts; they are blocked, fall short, and become powerless.

Can ambition that lusts after praise and position preach the gospel of him who made himself of no reputation and took upon himself the form of a servant – *who, being in the form of God, thought it not robbery to be equal with God, but emptied himself, taking the form of a slave, made in the likeness of men, and being found in fashion as a man, he humbled himself and became obedient unto death, even the death of the cross* (Philippians 2:6-8)?

Can the proud, the vain, or the egotistical preach the gospel of him who was meek and lowly? Can the bad-tempered, passionate, selfish, hard, worldly man preach a way that identifies with long-suffering, self-denial, and tenderness, and demands separation from and crucifixion to the world? Can the heartless, apathetic hireling preach the gospel that demands the shepherd give his life for the sheep?

Can the covetous man who counts his salary and money preach the gospel until he has gleaned his heart and can say in the spirit of Christ and Paul in the words of Wesley: "I count it dung and dross; I trample it under my feet; I (yet not I, but the grace of God in me) esteem it just as the mire of the street, I desire it not, I seek it not"? God's revelation does not need the light of human genius, the polish and strength of human culture, the brilliance of human thought, or the force of human brains to adorn or enforce it; but it does demand the simplicity, obedience, humility, and faith of a child's heart.

This surrender and subordination of intellect and genius to the divine and spiritual force made Paul unrivaled among the apostles, for he told the Romans to not *present your members as instruments of unrighteousness unto sin, but present yourselves unto God as those that are alive from the dead and your members as instruments of righteousness unto God* (Romans 6:13). This is what gave Wesley his power and established his labors in the history of humanity. This gave Loyola the strength to arrest the retreating forces of Catholicism.

Our great need is heart preparation. Luther held it as an axiom: "He who has prayed well has studied well." We do not say that men are not to think and use their intellects, but he will use his intellect best who cultivates his heart most. We do not say that preachers should not be students, but we do say that their great study should be the Bible, and he studies the Bible best who has kept his heart with diligence. We do not say that the preacher should not know men, but he will be more adept with human nature if he has discerned the depths and intricacies of his own heart.

> While the channel of preaching is the mind, its fountain is the heart.

We do say that while the channel of preaching is the mind, its fountain is the heart. You may broaden and deepen the channel, but if you do not care for the purity and depth of the fountain, you will have a dry or polluted channel. We do say that almost any man of common intelligence has sense enough to preach the gospel, but very few have grace enough to do so. We do say that he who has struggled with his own heart and conquered it has taken the first step of succeeding as a preacher. If he has taught his heart humility, faith, love, truth, mercy, sympathy, and courage, and can pour the rich treasures of his heart through a manly intellect that is surcharged with the power of the gospel, he will be the truest, most successful preacher in the favor of his Lord.

> *For God has not given us the spirit of fear, but of strength and of love and of temperance. Therefore be not thou ashamed to give testimony of our Lord, nor of me his prisoner, but be thou partaker of the afflictions of the gospel by the power of God, who has saved us and called us with a holy calling, not according to our works, but according to his own purpose and grace, which was given us in Christ Jesus before the times of the ages.* (2 Timothy 1:7-9)

Chapter 13

Working from the Heart

For with the heart one believes unto righteousness, and with the mouth confession is made unto saving health. – Romans 10:10

Study not to be a fine preacher. Jerichos are blown down with rams' horns. Look simply unto Jesus for preaching food; and what is wanted will be given, and what is given will be blessed, whether it is a barley grain or a wheat loaf, a crust or a crumb. Your mouth will be a flowing stream or a sealed fountain, according as your heart is. Avoid all controversy in preaching, talking or writing; preach nothing down but the devil, and nothing up but Jesus Christ.
– Berridge

The heart is the savior of the world. Heads do not save. Genius, brains, brilliance, strength, and natural gifts do not save. The gospel flows through hearts. All the mightiest forces are heart forces. All the sweetest and loveliest graces are heart graces. Great hearts make great characters; great hearts make divine characters.

God is love, and nothing is greater than love; nothing is greater than God. Hearts make heaven; heaven is love. There is nothing higher, nothing sweeter, than heaven. The heart and not the head makes God's great preachers. The heart rates high in every way in religion. The heart must speak from the pulpit. The heart must hear in the pew. In fact, we serve God with our hearts. Head homage or allegiance does not hit the mark in heaven.

We believe that one of the serious and most popular errors of the modern pulpit is putting more thought than prayer, more head than heart, in its sermons. Big hearts make big preachers; good hearts make good preachers. A theological school to enlarge and cultivate the heart is the golden fundamental of the gospel. The pastor binds his people to him and rules his people by his heart. They may admire his gifts, they may be proud of his ability, they may be affected for the time by his sermons; but the stronghold of his power is his heart. His scepter is love. The throne of his power is his heart.

The good shepherd gives his life for the sheep. Jesus said, *I AM the good shepherd; the good shepherd gives his life for the sheep* (John 10:11). Heads never make martyrs. The heart that surrenders the life to love and faithfulness makes martyrs. It takes great courage to be a faithful pastor, but the heart alone can supply this courage. Gifts and genius may be brave, but it is the gifts and genius of the heart and not of the head.

It is easier to fill the head than it is to prepare the heart. It is easier to make a brain sermon than a heart sermon. It was heart that drew the Son of God from heaven. It is heart that will draw men to heaven. Men of heart are what the world needs to sympathize with its woes, to kiss away its sorrows, to understand its misery, and to alleviate its pain. Christ was eminently the Man of Sorrows because he was preeminently the man of heart. He was *despised and rejected among men; a man of sorrows, and acquainted with weakness; and we hid as it were our faces from him; he was despised, and we esteemed him not. Surely he has borne our sicknesses and suffered our pain: and we considered him stricken, smitten of God, and cast down. But he was wounded for our rebellions; he was bruised for our iniquities; the chastisement of our peace was upon him; and by his stripes healing was provided for us* (Isaiah 53:3-5).

"Give me thy heart" is God's requisition of men. "Give me thy heart" is man's demand of man.

A professional ministry is a heartless ministry. When salary plays a great part in the ministry, the heart plays little part. We may make preaching our business and not put our hearts into the business. He who puts self to the front in his preaching puts heart to the rear. He who does not sow with his heart in his study will never reap a harvest for God. The prayer closet is the heart's study. We will learn more about how to preach and what to preach there than we can learn in our libraries. *Jesus wept* is the shortest and biggest verse in the

Bible (John 11:35). *He that goes forth and weeps* [not preaching great sermons], *bearing the precious seed, shall doubtless come again with rejoicing, bringing his sheaves with him* (Psalm 126:6).

Praying gives sense, brings wisdom, and broadens and strengthens the mind. The closet is a perfect schoolteacher and schoolhouse for the preacher. Thought is not only brightened and clarified in prayer, but thought is also born in prayer. We can learn more in an hour of prayer, when praying indeed, than from many hours in the study. Books in the prayer closet can be found and read nowhere else. Revelations are made in the closet, which are made nowhere else.

Call unto me, and I will answer thee and show thee great and difficult things, which thou dost not know. (Jeremiah 33:3)

Chapter 14

The Necessity of Anointing

I will ask the Father, and he shall give you another Comforter, that he may abide with you for ever, even the Spirit of truth, whom the world cannot receive because it does not see him, or know him; but ye know him, for he dwells with you and shall be in you. – John 14:16-17

One bright benediction which private prayer brings upon the ministry is an indescribable and unparalleled something – an anointing from the Holy One. If the anointing that we have does not come from the Lord of hosts, we are deceivers ... Let us continue instant, constant, and fervent in supplication. Let your fleece lie on the thrashing floor of supplication until it is wet with the dew of heaven. – Spurgeon

Alexander Knox, a Christian philosopher in the days of Wesley, not an adherent but a strong personal friend of Wesley's, had much spiritual sympathy with the Wesleyan movement. He writes:

It is strange and lamentable, but I believe that except among Methodists and Methodistical clergymen, there is not much interesting preaching in England. The clergy have absolutely lost the art. In the great laws of the moral world, there is a kind of secret understanding like the affinities in chemistry, between rightly circulated religious truth and the deepest feelings of the human mind. Where the one is duly exhibited, the other will respond – did not our hearts burn within us? But this devout feeling is indispensable in the speaker.

Now, I am obliged to state from my own observation that this anointing is beyond all comparison more likely to be found in England in a Methodist meeting house than in a parish church. This, and this alone, seems to be what fills the Methodist houses and thins the churches. I believe I am no enthusiast; I am a most sincere and cordial churchman, a humble disciple of the School of Hale and Boyle, of Burnet and Leighton. Now I must aver that when I was in this country two years ago, I did not hear a single preacher who taught me like my own great masters but such as are deemed Methodist. And I now despair of getting an ounce of heart instruction from any other quarter. The Methodist preachers (though I may not always approve of all their expressions) do most assuredly dispense this true, undefiled religion. I felt real pleasure last Sunday. I can bear witness that the preacher did speak the words of truth and soberness. There was no eloquence; the honest man never dreamed of such a thing, but there was far better – a cordial communication of vitalized truth. I say vitalized because what he declared to others was impossible not to feel he lived himself.

This anointing is the art of preaching. The preacher who never had this never had the art of preaching. The preacher who has lost it has lost the art of preaching. Whatever other arts he may have and retain – the art of making a sermon, the art of eloquence, the art of great, clear thinking, and the art of pleasing an audience – if he has lost the anointing, he has lost the divine art of preaching, because it makes God's truth powerful and interesting. It draws and attracts, edifies, convicts, and saves.

This spirituality vitalizes God's revealed truth and makes it living and life giving. God's truth spoken without this divineness is light, dead, and deadening. Though abounding in truth, weighty with thought, sparkling with rhetoric, pointed by logic, and powerful by earnestness, without this sacredness, it hastens in death and not in life. Mr. Spurgeon says:

> I wonder how long we might beat our brains before we could plainly put into words what is meant by preaching with anointing. Yet he who preaches knows its presence, and he who hears soon detects its absence. In famine, Samaria

typifies a discourse without it. With her feast of fat things full of marrow, Jerusalem may represent a sermon enriched with it. Everyone knows what the freshness of the morning is when diamonds abound on every blade of grass; but who can describe it, much less produce it of itself? Such is the mystery of spiritual anointing. We know, but we cannot tell others what it is. It is as easy to counterfeit as it is foolish. Anointing is something that you cannot manufacture, and its counterfeits are less than worthless. Yet it is, in itself, priceless and beyond measure but needful if you want to edify believers and bring sinners to Christ.

But the anointing which ye have received of him abides in you, and ye do not need that anyone teach you; but as the same anointing teaches you of all things and is truth, and is no lie; and even as it has taught you, abide ye in him.
(1 John 2:27)

Chapter 15

Anointed Preaching

Preach the word; be instant in season and out of season; reprove, rebuke, exhort with all longsuffering and doctrine. – 2 Timothy 4:2

Speak for eternity. Above all things, cultivate your own spirit. A word spoken by you when your conscience is clear and your heart full of God's Spirit is worth ten thousand words spoken in unbelief and sin. Remember that God, and not man, must have the glory. If the veil of the world's machinery were lifted off, how much we would find is done in answer to the prayers of God's children. – Robert Murray McCheyne

The anointing is that indefinable, indescribable something (Holy Spirit) that an old, renowned Scottish preacher describes thus: "There is sometimes something in preaching that cannot be ascribed either to matter or expression and cannot be described as to what it is or from whence it comes. *The wind blows where it desires, and thou hearest the sound of it, but canst not tell from where it comes or where it goes; so is every one that is born of the Spirit* (John 3:8). But with a sweet force, it pierces into the heart and affections and comes immediately from the Lord. If there were any way to obtain such a thing, it is the heavenly disposition of the speaker."

We call this an anointing that empowers the preacher: *the word of God is alive and efficient and sharper than any twoedged sword, piercing even to the dividing asunder of soul and spirit, and of the joints and marrow, and is a discerner of the thoughts and intents of the heart* (Hebrews 4:12). This divine influence gives the words of the preacher conciseness, sharpness, and power, and creates conflict and uneasiness in many a dead congregation. The same truths have been told in the strictness of the letter, smooth as human oil could make them, but without any signs of life or pulse throbs in the hearts; all were as peaceful as the grave and as dead. The same preacher in the meantime might receive an anointing; the divine inspiration comes on him, and the letter of the Word is embellished and fired by this mysterious power, and the throbbings of life begin – life which receives or life which resists. The Holy Spirit penetrates and convicts the conscience and breaks the heart.

This divine anointing is the feature which separates and distinguishes true gospel preaching from all other methods of presenting the truth, and which creates a wide spiritual chasm between the preacher who has it and the one who does not. It supports and saturates revealed truth with all the energy of God. Anointing is simply putting God into his own Word and on his own preacher. By mighty and great prayerfulness and by continued prayerfulness, God and his Word become the potential to the preacher personally. They inspire and clarify his intellect, give insight, and grasp projecting power. God gives the preacher heart power, which is greater than head power; tenderness, purity, and force flow from the heart of the God-empowered preacher. Enlargement, freedom, fullness of thought, directness, and simplicity of utterance are the fruits of this close association to the Holy Spirit.

> God gives the preacher heart power, which is greater than head power.

Often earnestness is mistaken for this anointing. He who has the divine blessedness will be earnest in the very spiritual nature of things, but a vast deal of earnestness may be without this same spirituality.

Earnestness and anointing look alike from some points of view. Earnestness may be readily and without detection substituted or mistaken for anointing. It requires a spiritual eye and a spiritual taste to discern the difference.

Earnestness may be sincere, serious, passionate, and persevering. It approaches things with good will, pursues with perseverance, urges with zeal, and puts force toward it. But all of these forces do not rise higher than the mere human. The man is doing the work, the whole man, with all that he has of will and heart, of brain and genius, of planning and working and talking. He sets himself to some purpose that has mastered him, and he pursues mastering it. This work may not be of God. There may be little of God in it, because there is so much of the man in it. He may present pleas as an advocate of his earnest purpose, which please or touch and move or overwhelm with conviction of their importance. In all this earnestness, he may move along earthly ways, being propelled by human forces, its altar made by earthly hands and its fire kindled by earthly flames.

It is said that a rather famous preacher of gifts used Scripture to his fancy or purpose, and he "grew very eloquent over his own exegesis." So men grow exceedingly earnest over their own plans or movements. Earnestness may be selfishness in disguise.

What of anointing? It is the indefinable in preaching that makes it preaching. It is that which distinguishes and separates preaching from all mere human addresses. It is the divine in preaching. It makes the preaching sharp to those who need sharpness. It purifies as the dew to those who need to be refreshed. It is well described as:

> A two-edged sword
>   Of heavenly temper keen,
> And double were the wounds it made
>   Where'er it glanced between.
> 'Twas death to sin; 'twas life
>   To all who mourned for sin.
> It kindled and it silenced strife,
>   Made war and peace within.

This anointing comes to the preacher in the prayer closet, not in the study. It is heaven's distillation in answer to prayer. It is the sweetest exhaling of the Holy Spirit.

It saturates, permeates, softens, penetrates, cuts, and soothes. It carries the Word like dynamite, like salt, and like sugar; it makes the Word a soother, an accuser, a revealer, and a searcher. It makes the hearer a culprit or a saint; it makes him weep like a child and live like a giant. It opens his heart and his purse as gently, yet as strongly, as the spring opens the leaves.

This anointing is not the gift of genius. It is not found in the halls of learning, and no eloquence can woo it. No industry can win it; no ecclesiastical hands can confer it. It is the gift of God – the seal to his own messengers. It is heaven's knighthood given to the chosen true and brave ones, often the same ones who have sought this anointed honor through many an hour of tearful, wrestling prayer.

Earnestness is good and impressive; genius is gifted and great; thought kindles and inspires, but it takes a more blessed endowment, a more powerful energy than earnestness or genius or thought to break the chains of sin, win estranged and depraved hearts to God, repair the breaches, and restore the church to her old ways of purity and power. Nothing but the Holy Spirit can do this.

> *God is a Spirit and those that worship him must worship him in spirit and in truth.* (John 4:24)

Chapter 16

Genuine Anointing

Now we have not received the spirit of the world, but the Spirit which is of God, that we might know the things that God has given us. Which things also we speak, not in the words which man's wisdom teaches, but with doctrine of the Holy Spirit, jointly fitting spiritual things by spiritual means. – 1 Corinthians 2:12-13

All the minister's efforts will be vanity or worse than vanity if he does not have the Holy Spirit. He must come down from heaven and spread a savor and feeling and relish over his ministry. Among the other means of qualifying himself for his office, the Bible must hold the first place, and the last place must also be given to the Word of God and prayer. – Richard Cecil

In the Christian system, the anointing comes from the Holy Spirit; he separates and qualifies men for God's work. This anointing is the one divine enablement by which the preacher accomplishes the peculiar purpose of preaching. Without it there are no true spiritual results accomplished; the results and forces in preaching do not rise above the results of unsanctified speech. Without it the forum is as impotent as the pulpit.

This divine anointing on the preacher generates spiritual results that flow from the gospel through the Word of God. Without this anointing, these results are not secured. But *our gospel did not come unto you in word only, but also in power and in the Holy Spirit and in full assurance as ye know what manner of men we were among you for your sake* (1 Thessalonians 1:5).

Many pleasant impressions may be made, but they fall far below the purpose of gospel preaching. This anointing may be mimicked. Many things can look like it, and many results can resemble its effects, but they are counterfeit results and appearances. The intensity or softness produced by a pathetic or emotional sermon may look like the movements of the Holy Spirit, but they have no piercing, penetrating, heartbreaking force. No heart-healing balm emerges in these shallow, sympathetic, emotional movements; they are not radical, sin searching, or sin curing.

This Holy Spirit is the one distinguishing feature that separates true gospel preaching from all other methods of presenting truth. *When he, the Spirit of truth, is come, he will guide you into all truth* (John 16:13). It supports and reinforces the revealed truth with all the force of God. It illumines the Word as it broadens and enriches the intellect and empowers it to grasp and comprehend the Word. It enables the preacher's heart and brings it to the point of tenderness, purity, force, and light that are necessary to accomplish the highest results. The Holy Spirit gives the preacher liberty and understanding, and the soul receives freedom and fullness that can be obtained by no other process.

Without this anointing on the preacher, the gospel has no more power to multiply itself than any other system of truth. This is the seal of its divinity. The Holy Spirit in the preacher puts God in the gospel. Without the Holy Spirit, God is absent, and the gospel is left to the low and unsatisfactory forces that the ingenuity, interest, or talents of men can devise to enforce and project its doctrines.

> Without the Holy Spirit, God is absent, and the gospel is left to the unsatisfactory forces of the ingenuity, interest, or talents of men.

It is in this element that the pulpit fails more often than any other element. It lapses at this all-important point. Knowledge may astonish; brilliance and eloquence may delight and charm; sensation or tactful methods may bring the crowds. Mental power may impress and enforce truth with all its resources, but without the Holy Spirit, each of these will only be as the grinding assault of the waters on Gibraltar. Spray and foam may cover and sparkle, but the rocks are still there, unimpressed and immovable. The human heart can no more be swept of its hardness and sin by these human forces than these rocks can be swept away by the ocean's ceaseless thrashing.

This anointing is the consecration force, and its presence is the continuous test of that holiness. This divine anointing on the preacher is what secures his devotion to God and his work. Other forces and motives may call him to the work, but only this is consecration. A separation to God's work by the power of the Holy Spirit is the only consecration recognized by God as legitimate.

This heavenly anointing is what the pulpit needs and must have. This divine and heavenly oil applied by God's hand must soften the whole man – heart, head, and spirit – until it separates him with a mighty separation from all earthly, secular, worldly, and selfish motives and goals. It will separate him to everything that is pure and godlike.

The presence of this anointing on the preacher creates a turmoil and agitation in many congregations. The same truths have been told in the strictness of the letter, but no ruffle has appeared, no pain or pulsation felt. All is quiet as a graveyard. Another preacher comes, and this mysterious influence is on him; the letter of the Word has been fired by the Spirit, and the throes of a mighty movement are felt. The Holy Spirit is what pervades and stirs the conscience and breaks the heart. Spiritless preaching makes everything hard, dry, acrid, and dead.

This anointing is not only a memory or an era of the past, but it is also a present, realized, conscious fact. It belongs to the experience of the man as well as to his preaching. It is that which transforms him into the image of his divine Master, as well as that by which he declares the truths of Christ with power. This anointing is the power in the ministry to make all else seem insignificant and vain, and by its presence to make up for the absence of all other techniques and programs.

This anointing is a conditional gift, and its presence is perpetuated and increased by the same process by which it was at first secured – by unceasing prayer to God, by impassioned desires after God, by seeking it with tireless passion, and by deeming all else loss and failure without it.

This anointing comes directly from God in answer to prayer or by the laying on of hands of those who pray. Only praying hearts are hearts filled with this holy oil; only praying lips are anointed in this way.

Prayer, much prayer, is the price of anointed preaching; prayer, much prayer, is the one condition of keeping this blessing. Without unceasing prayer, the anointing never comes to the preacher. Without perseverance in prayer, the anointing, like the day-old manna, breeds worms.

And I was with you in weakness and in fear and in much trembling. And my speech and my preaching was not with enticing words of human wisdom, but in demonstration of the Spirit and of power, that your faith should not be founded in the wisdom of men, but in the power of God.
(1 Corinthians 2:3-5)

Chapter 17

Spiritual Leaders Pray

Abide in me, and I in you. As the branch cannot bear fruit of itself, except it abides in the vine, no more can ye, except ye abide in me. In this is my Father clarified in that ye bear much fruit; and in this manner ye shall be my disciples.
– John 15:4, 8

Give me one hundred preachers who fear nothing but sin and desire nothing but God, and I care not a straw whether they be clergymen or laymen; such alone will shake the gates of hell and set up the kingdom of heaven on earth. God does nothing but in answer to prayer.
– John Wesley

The apostles knew the necessity and worth of prayer to their ministry. They knew that their high commission as apostles, instead of relieving them of the necessity of prayer, committed them to it by a more urgent need. They were exceedingly jealous that some other important work would not exhaust their time and prevent their praying as they needed. They appointed laymen to look after the delicate and time-consuming duties of ministering to the poor, so they (the apostles) might give themselves *continually to prayer and to the ministry of the word* (Acts 6:4). Prayer is put first, and their relationship to prayer is put most strongly: *give ourselves* to it, making a business of it, surrendering themselves to praying, and putting intensity, urgency, perseverance, and time into it.

How holy, apostolic men devoted themselves to this divine work of prayer: *night and day praying exceedingly*, says Paul (1 Thessalonians 3:10). *We will give ourselves continually to prayer* is the consensus of apostolic devotion. How these New Testament preachers laid themselves out in prayer for God's people! How they put God in full force into their churches by their praying! These holy apostles did not proudly assume that they had met their high and solemn duties by delivering God's Word faithfully, but their preaching was made to adhere and endure by the passion and persistence of their praying.

Apostolic praying was as taxing, toilsome, and imperative as apostolic preaching. They prayed mightily day and night to bring their people to the highest levels of faith and holiness. As Paul said, *I thank my God upon every remembrance of you always in every prayer of mine for you all, making request with joy, for your fellowship in the gospel from the first day until now* (Philippians 1:3-5). They prayed mightier still to hold the people to this high spiritual altitude. The preacher who has never learned the high and divine art of intercession for his people will never learn the art of preaching, even though homiletics might be poured into him by the ton, and he might be the most-gifted genius in making and delivering sermons.

The prayers of apostolic, saintly leaders do much in making saints of those who are not apostles. If the later church leaders had been as particular and fervent in praying for their people as the apostles were, the sad, dark times of worldliness and apostasy would not have marred the history, eclipsed the glory, and arrested the advance of the church. Apostolic praying makes apostolic saints and keeps apostolic times of purity and power in the church.

> The preacher must devote himself to prayer for his people – not that they might be simply saved, but that they might be mightily saved.

What loftiness of soul, what purity and elevation of motive, what unselfishness, what self-sacrifice, what exhaustive toil, what passionate spirit, and what divine tact are required to be an intercessor for men!

The preacher must devote himself to prayer for his people – not that they might be simply saved, but that they might be mightily saved. The apostles dedicated themselves to prayer that their saints might be perfect – not that they would have a little relish for the things of God, but that they *might be filled with all the fullness of God* (Ephesians 3:19). Paul did not rely on his apostolic preaching to secure this end, but he said, *for this cause I bow my knees unto the Father of our Lord Jesus Christ* (Ephesians 3:14). Paul's praying carried Paul's converts further along the highway of sainthood than Paul's preaching did. Epaphras did as much or more by prayer for the Colossian saints than by his preaching. He labored fervently always in prayer for them that they might *stand firm, perfect and fulfilled in all the will of God* (Colossians 4:12).

Preachers are preeminently God's leaders. They are primarily responsible for the condition of the church, for they shape its character and give tone and direction to its life.

Much in every way depends on these leaders. They shape the times and the institutions. The church is divine, and the treasure it encases is heavenly, but it bears the imprint of the human. The treasure is in earthen vessels, and it resembles the vessel. The church of God makes, or is made by, its leaders. Whether it makes them or is made by them, it will be what its leaders are – spiritual if they are spiritual, secular if they are secular, convoluted if its leaders are convoluted.

Israel's kings gave character to Israel's allegiance. A church rarely revolts against or rises above the religion of its leaders. Strong spiritual leaders, men of holy might at the lead, are tokens of God's favor; disaster and weakness follow the wake of weak or worldly leaders. Israel had fallen low, so God gave children to be their princes and babes to rule over them. No happy state is predicted by the prophets when children oppress God's Israel and women rule over them. Times of spiritual leadership are times of great spiritual prosperity for the church.

Prayer is one of the distinguished characteristics of strong spiritual leadership. Men of mighty prayer are men of might who mold things. Their power with God has the conquering tread.

How can a man preach if he does not get his message fresh from God in the prayer closet? How can he preach without having his faith quickened, his vision cleared, and his heart warmed by his solitude with God? Alas, for the pulpit lips are untouched by this closet flame. Dry and spiritless they will ever be, and divine truths will never come with power from such lips. As far as the real interests of religion are concerned, a pulpit without a prayer closet will always be a barren thing.

> A pulpit without a prayer closet will always be a barren thing.

A preacher may preach in an official, entertaining, or learned way without prayer, but between this kind of preaching and sowing God's precious seed with holy hands and prayerful weeping hearts, is an immeasurable distance.

A prayerless ministry is the undertaker for all God's truth and for God's church. It may have the most costly casket and the most beautiful flowers, but it is a funeral, notwithstanding the charming array. A prayerless Christian will never learn God's truth; a prayerless ministry will never be able to teach God's truth. Ages of millennial glory have been lost by a prayerless church. The coming of our Lord has been postponed indefinitely by a prayerless church. Hell has enlarged herself and filled her dire caves in the presence of the dead service of a prayerless church.

The best and the greatest offering is an offering of

prayer. If the preachers of the twentieth century would learn the lesson of prayer and use the power of prayer, the millennium will come to its high point before the century closes. *Pray without ceasing* is the trumpet call to the preachers of the twentieth century. If they will get their texts, their thoughts, their words, and their sermons in their prayer closets, the next century will find a new heaven and a new earth. The old sin-stained and sin-eclipsed heaven and earth will pass away under the power of a praying ministry.

> *Praying always with all prayer and supplication in the Spirit and watching in this with all perseverance and supplication for all the saints.* (Ephesians 6:18)

Chapter 18

Prayer for the Preacher

Listen to your pastors, and do not resist them, for they watch for your souls as those that must give account, that they may do it with joy, and not with grief; for that is unprofitable for you. Pray for us: for we trust we have a good conscience in all things desiring to conduct ourselves well. – Hebrews 13:17-18

If some Christians that have been complaining of their ministers had said and acted less before men and had applied themselves with all their might to cry to God for their ministers and had arisen and stormed heaven with their humble, fervent, and incessant prayers for them, they would have been much more in the way of success. – Jonathan Edwards

Somehow the practice of praying in particular for the preacher has been neglected or discounted. Occasionally we have heard the practice denounced as derogatory toward the ministry and proclaimed it a declaration of the inefficiency of the ministry. Perhaps it offends the pride of learning and self-sufficiency, but these ought to be offended and rebuked in a ministry that is so derelict as to allow that pride to exist.

To the preacher, prayer is not simply the duty of his profession and a privilege, but it is a necessity. Air is not more necessary to the lungs than prayer is to the preacher. It is absolutely necessary for the preacher to pray, and it is an absolute necessity that the preacher be prayed for. These two essentials are wedded into a union that should never see divorce: the preacher must pray, and the preacher must be prayed for. It will take all the praying he can do, and all the praying he can get, to meet the fearful responsibilities and gain the largest, truest success in his great work. Next to the cultivation of the spirit and fact of prayer in himself, the true preacher covets with a great covetousness the prayers of God's people in their deepest form.

The holier a man is, the more he values prayer and the clearer he sees that God gives himself to the praying ones. The measure of God's revelation to the soul is the measure of the soul's longing, persistent prayer for God. Salvation never finds its way to a prayerless heart. The Holy Spirit never abides in a prayerless spirit. Preaching never edifies a prayerless soul; Christ knows nothing of prayerless Christians.

The gospel cannot be projected by a prayerless preacher. Gifts, talents, education, eloquence, or God's call cannot reduce the demand for prayer; they only intensify the necessity for the preacher to pray and to be prayed for. The more the preacher's eyes are opened to the nature, responsibility, and difficulties in his work, the more he will see, and if he is a true preacher, the more he will feel the necessity of prayer – not only the increasing demand to pray himself, but also to call on others to pray for him.

Paul is an illustration of this. If any man could project the gospel by personal force, brainpower, culture, personal grace, God's apostolic commission, or God's extraordinary call, that man was Paul. He is an eminent example that the preacher must be a man given to prayer. He is also a preeminent example that the true apostolic preacher must have the prayers of good people to give success to his ministry.

Paul asks, he covets, he pleads in an impassioned way for the help of all God's saints. He knew that in the spiritual realm, as elsewhere, there is strength in union, and that the concentration and amassing of faith, desire, and prayer increased the spiritual force until it became overwhelming and irresistible in its power. Units of prayer merge, and like drops of water, make an ocean that defies resistance. So with his clear and full comprehension of spiritual dynamics, Paul determined to make his ministry as impressive, eternal, and irresistible as the ocean by gathering all the scattered units of prayer and precipitating them on his ministry. Is the reason for Paul's success his ability to impress on the church and the world his need for prayer? Was he able to center more prayer on himself than others?

To his brethren at Rome he wrote, *But I beseech you, brethren, by our Lord Jesus Christ, and by the charity of the Spirit, that ye help me with prayers to God for me* (Romans 15:30). To the Ephesians he said, *praying always with all prayer and supplication in the Spirit and watching in this with all perseverance and supplication for all saints and for me, that utterance may be given unto me, that I may open my mouth with confidence, to make known the mystery of the gospel* (Ephesians 6:18-19). To the Colossians he emphasized, *praying also together for us that God would open unto us the door of the word, to speak the mystery of the Christ, for which I am also in bonds, that I may make it manifest, as I ought to speak* (Colossians 4:3-4). To the Thessalonians he spoke strongly: *Brethren, pray for us* (1 Thessalonians 5:25). Paul calls on the Corinthian church to help him: *ye also helping us with prayer* (2 Corinthians 1:11).

This was to be part of their work – the helping hand of prayer. In an additional and closing charge to the Thessalonian church, he spoke about the importance and necessity of their prayers: *Finally, brethren, pray for us, that the word of the Lord may have free course and be glorified, even as it is with you, And that we may be delivered from perverse and wicked men* (2 Thessalonians 3:1-2). To the Philippians, he stressed that the effectiveness of their prayers for him for the spread of the gospel could make all his trials and opposition insignificant (Philippians 1:19). Philemon was to prepare a lodging for him, for through Philemon's prayer Paul was to be his guest (Philemon 1:22).

Paul's attitude in his need for prayer illustrates his

humility and his deep insight into the spiritual forces that advance the gospel. More than this, it teaches a lesson for all times: if Paul was so dependent on the prayers of God's saints to give his ministry success, how much more should God's saints center their ministry on prayer today!

Paul knew this urgent plea for prayer did not lower his dignity, lessen his influence, or depreciate his devotion. What if it did? Let dignity go, let influence be destroyed, let his reputation be marred – he must have their prayers. Called and commissioned as chief of the apostles as he was, all his resources were imperfect without the prayers of his people. He wrote letters everywhere and urged the people to pray for him.

Do you pray for your preacher? Do you pray for him in secret? Public prayers are of little worth unless they are founded on or followed up by private praying. The praying ones are to the preacher as Aaron and Hur were to Moses. They held his hands up as the battle raged around them:

> *Joshua did as Moses had said to him and fought with Amalek; and Moses, Aaron, and Hur went up to the top of the hill. And it came to pass, when Moses held up his hand, that Israel prevailed; but when he let down his hand, Amalek prevailed. And Moses' hands were heavy, so they took a stone and put it under him, and he sat upon it; and Aaron and Hur stayed up his hands, the one on the one side and the other on the other side; thus his hands were steady until*

the going down of the sun. And Joshua disabled Amalek and his people with the edge of the sword. (Exodus 17:10-13)

The plea and purpose of the apostles were to put the church to praying. They did not ignore the grace of cheerful giving. They were not ignorant of the place that religious activity and work had in the spiritual life, but not one of these could compare in necessity and importance with prayer. The most sacred and urgent pleas were used; the most intense exhortations and the most comprehensive and arousing words were uttered to emphasize the all-important obligation and necessity of prayer.

"Put the saints everywhere to praying" is the burden of the apostolic effort and the keynote of apostolic success. Jesus Christ had endeavored to do this in the days of his personal ministry. As he was moved by infinite compassion at the ripened fields of earth perishing for lack of laborers, he paused in his own praying and tried to awaken the stupid sensibilities of his disciples to the duty of prayer when he charged them: *pray ye therefore the Lord of the harvest, that he will send forth labourers into his harvest* (Matthew 9:38).

And he spoke a parable unto them to this end, that it behooves us always to pray and not faint. (Luke 18:1)

Chapter 19

Giving Yourself to Prayer

But ask in faith, not doubting anything. For he that doubts is like the wave of the sea which is driven of the wind and is tossed from one side to another. – James 1:6

This perpetual hurry of business and company ruins me in soul, if not in body. More solitude and earlier hours! I suspect I have been allotting too little time to religious exercises, as private devotion, religious meditation, and Scripture-reading. . . . I have been keeping too late hours, and hence have had but a hurried half hour in a morning to myself. Surely, . . . without a due measure of private devotions the soul will grow lean. But all may be done through prayer – almighty prayer. That it is almighty is only through the gracious arrangement of the God of love and truth. Oh, then, pray, pray, pray!
– William Wilberforce

Our devotions are not measured by the clock, but time is fundamental. The ability to wait and press on belongs essentially to our intercourse with God. To an alarming extent, hurry is damaging the great business of communion with God. Short devotions are the bane of deep adoration. Calmness, understanding, and strength are never the companions of hurry. Short devotions deplete spiritual life, arrest spiritual progress, sap spiritual foundations, and blight the root and bloom of spiritual life. They are the prolific source of backsliding, the sure indication of a superficial spirituality; they deceive, blight, rot the seed, and impoverish the soil.

It is true that Bible prayers in word and print are short, but the praying men of the Bible were with God through many sweet and holy wrestling hours. They won by few words but by prolonged waiting. The prayers Moses recorded may be short, but Moses prayed to God with fastings and mighty crying for forty days and nights.

The statement of Elijah's praying may be condensed to a few brief paragraphs, but doubtless Elijah, who, when "praying he prayed," spent many hours of fiery struggle and lofty communion with God before he could say with assured boldness to Ahab, *there shall not be dew nor rain these years, but according to my word* (1 Kings 17:1). The verbal brief of Paul's prayers is short, but Paul prayed *night and day praying exceedingly* (1 Thessalonians 3:10). The Lord's Prayer is a divine summary for infant lips, but the man Christ Jesus often prayed all night before his work was done. His all-night and long-sustained devotions gave his work its finish and perfection; they gave his character the fullness and glory of its divinity.

Spiritual work is taxing work, and men are reluctant to do it. Praying – true praying – requires an investment of serious attention and time, which flesh and blood do not relish. Few people are made of such strong fiber that they will commit to such an undertaking when surface work will pass as well in the market. We can devote ourselves to our beggarly praying until it looks sufficient to us – at least it keeps up a decent form and quiets the conscience – the deadliest of opiates! We can slight our praying and not realize the peril until the foundations are gone. Hurried devotions make weak faith, wavering convictions, and questionable reverence. To be little with God is to be little for God. To cut the praying short makes the whole religious character short, scant, selfish, and slovenly.

> To be little with God is to be little for God.

It takes time for the full flow of God to get into the spirit. Short devotions cut the pipe of God's flow short. It takes time in the secret places to get the full revelation of God. Little time and hurry mar the picture.

Henry Martyn lamented, "Lack of private devotional reading and shortness of prayer through unending sermon development had produced much strangeness between God and his soul." He judged that he had dedicated too much time to public services and too little to private communion with God. He was convicted to set aside times for fasting and devotion times for solemn prayer. Resulting from this, he recorded, "Was assisted this morning to pray for two hours."

William Wilberforce, the peer of kings, said, "I

must secure more time for private devotions. I have been living far too public for me. The shortening of private devotions starves the soul; it grows lean and faint. I have been keeping too late hours." Of a failure in Parliament he said, "Let me record my grief and shame, and all, probably, from private devotions having been shortened; so God let me stumble." More solitude and earlier hours was his remedy.

More time and early hours for prayer will revive and invigorate many decayed spiritual lives. More time and early hours for prayer embody holy living. A holy life would not be so rare or so difficult a thing if our devotions were not so short and hurried. A Christlike temper in its sweet and passionless fragrance would not be so alien and hopeless a heritage if our prayer-closet time was lengthened and intensified. We live shabbily because we pray poorly. Plenty of time feasting in our prayer closets will bring spiritual marrow and fatness to our lives. Our ability to stay with God in solitude measures our ability to stay with God in public. Hasty prayer times are deceptive and defaulting. We are not only deluded by them, but we are also losers by them in many ways and in many rich legacies.

> Plenty of time feasting in our prayer closets will bring spiritual marrow and fatness to our lives.

Lingering in the closet instructs and wins. The greatest victories are often the result of great waiting – waiting until words and plans are exhausted, and silent, patient waiting gains the crown. *Be silent before the LORD and wait patiently for him* (Psalm 37:7). Jesus

Christ asked with emphasis, *shall not God avenge his own elect who cry day and night unto him?* (Luke 18:7).

To pray is the greatest thing we can do, and to do it well there must be calmness, time, and deliberation. Otherwise it is degraded into the littlest and most common of things. True praying has the greatest results for good, and poor praying, the least. We cannot do too much of real praying; we cannot do too little of the phony sham. We must learn again the worth of prayer and enter again the school of prayer. There is nothing that takes more time to learn. And if we would learn this wondrous art, we must not give a fragment here and there – "A Little Talk with Jesus," as the children sing. We must demand and hold with iron fists the best hours of the day for God and prayer, or there will be no praying worth recognizing.

This, however, is not a day of prayer. Few men pray. Prayer is defamed by preacher and priest. In these days of hurry and bustle, electricity and steam, men will not take time to pray. There are preachers who "say prayers" as a part of their program on regular, set occasions, but who "revives himself to take hold upon God?" Who prays as Jacob prayed – until he is crowned as a prevailing, princely intercessor? Who prays as Elijah prayed – until all the locked-up forces of nature were unsealed and a famine-stricken land bloomed as the garden of God? Who prays as Jesus Christ prayed when *he went out into the mountain to pray and continued all night in prayer to God* (Luke 6:12)?

The apostles "gave themselves to prayer" – the most difficult thing to get men or even the preachers to do.

There are laymen who will give their money, some of them in rich abundance, but they will not "give themselves" to prayer, without which their money is but a curse. Plenty of preachers will preach and deliver great and eloquent addresses on the need of revival and the spread of the kingdom of God, but not many will do that thing without which all preaching and organizing are worse than vain – pray. Prayer is out of date, almost a lost art, and the greatest benefactor this age could have is the man who will bring the preachers and the church back to prayer.

> *I thank my God upon every remembrance of you always in every prayer of mine for you all, making request with joy.* (Philippians 1:3-4)

Chapter 20

A Praying Pulpit Begets a Praying Pew

[I] cease not to give thanks for you, making mention of you in my prayers; that the God of our Lord Jesus Christ, the Father of glory, may give unto you the spirit of wisdom and revelation in the knowledge of him; illuminating the eyes of your understanding, that ye may know what is the hope of his calling and what are the riches of the glory of his inheritance in the saints and what is the exceeding greatness of his power in us who believe. – Ephesians 1:16-19

I judge that my prayer is more than the devil himself; if it were otherwise, Luther would have fared differently long before this. Yet men will not see and acknowledge the great wonders or miracles God works in my behalf. If I should neglect prayer but a single day, I should lose a great deal of the fire of faith. – Martin Luther

The apostles could only get glimpses of the great importance of prayer before Pentecost. But when the Spirit came and filled the people on Pentecost, prayer was elevated to its vital and allcommanding position in the gospel of Christ. The call now to every saint is the Spirit's loudest and most urgent call. Sanctification is made, refined, and perfected by prayer. The gospel moves at a slow and timid pace when the saints are not at their prayers early and late and for a long time.

Where are the Christlike leaders who can teach the modern saints how to pray and set them to do it? Do we realize we are raising up a prayerless set of saints? Where are the apostolic leaders who can put God's people to praying? Let them come to the front and do the work, and it will be the greatest work that can be done. An increase of educational facilities and a great increase of money will be the direst curse to religion if believers are not sanctified by more and better praying than we are doing. More praying will not come automatically. The campaign for the twentieth- or thirtieth-century fund will not help our praying, but it will hinder it if we are not careful.

Nothing but a specific effort from a praying leadership will accomplish this. The chief ones must lead in the apostolic effort to emphasize the vital importance and fact of prayer in the heart and life of the church. No one but praying leaders can have praying followers. Praying apostles will beget praying saints. A praying pulpit will beget praying pews.

We do greatly need somebody who can set the saints to this business of praying. We are not a generation of praying saints. Non-praying saints are a beggarly gang of saints who have no passion, no beauty, and no power of saints. Who will restore this breach? The one who can set the church to praying will be the greatest of reformers and apostles.

Our most sober judgment is that the great need of the church is men of such commanding faith – men of unsullied holiness, marked spiritual eagerness, and consuming zeal. Their prayers, faith, lives, and ministry will be of such a radical and aggressive form as to work spiritual revolutions that will form eras in individual and church life.

We do not mean men who stir up sensational emotions by novel devices or those who attract by pleasing entertainment. We need men who can stir things and work revolutions by the preaching of God's Word and by the power of the Holy Spirit, revolutions that change all the current trends.

Natural ability and educational advantages do not figure as factors in this matter. Capacity for faith, the ability to pray, the power of thorough consecration, and the ability of humility are needed. Men must lose themselves in God's glory and retain an ever-present, insatiable yearning, as they seek after all the fullness of God. *As the hart pants after the water brooks, so does my soul pant after thee, O God. My soul thirsts for God, for the living God* (Psalm 42:1-2). Men who yearn for God like this can set the church ablaze – not in a noisy, showy way, but with an intense and quiet heat that melts and moves everything for God.

> Men can work wonders if they can get God to lead them.

God can work wonders if he can get a suitable man.

Men can work wonders if they can get God to lead them. The full endowment of the spirit that turned the world upside down would be exceedingly useful in these latter days. Men who can stir things mightily for God, whose spiritual revolutions change the whole direction of things, are the universal need of the church.

The church has never been without these men; they adorn its history; they are the standing miracles of the divinity of the church. Their example and history are an unfailing inspiration and blessing. We should pray for an increase in their number and power.

That which has been done in spiritual matters can be done again and can be done better. This was Christ's view. He said, *Verily, verily, I say unto you, He that believes in me, the works that I do he shall do also; and greater works than these shall he do because I go unto my Father* (John 14:12). The past has not exhausted the possibilities or the demands for doing great things for God. The church that is dependent on its history for its miracles of power and grace is a fallen church.

God wants elect men – men who have experienced a severe crucifixion of self and have totally ruined their selves and the world so that there is neither hope nor desire of recovery. God wants men who have turned perfect hearts toward him.

Let us pray passionately that God's promise to prayer may be more than realized.

> *Persevere in prayer and watch in the same with thanksgiving.* (Colossians 4:2)

E. M. Bounds – A Short Biography

Edward McKendree Bounds was born in Shelby County, Missouri, on August 15, 1835, and died on August 24, 1913, in Washington, Georgia. He was admitted to the bar in 1854 at the age of nineteen, but left the profession five years later when he answered the call of God to the ministry. Beginning in 1863, in the midst of the Civil War, he became the chaplain of the Fifth Missouri Regiment of the Confederacy.

Bounds married Miss Emmie Barnett of Eufaula, Alabama, in 1876. By this union, he became the father of two daughters, Celeste and Corneille, and a son, Edward, who died at the age of six. His wife Emmie died in 1886, and later Bounds married Miss Hattie Barnett, Emmie's cousin. Together they had six children: Samuel, Charles, Osborne, Elizabeth, Mary, and Emmie. However, Charles died at the age of one, so in the end, the family consisted of seven children.[1]

After serving several important churches in St.

---

1 Lyle Wesley Dorsett, *E. M. Bounds: Man of Prayer* (Grand Rapids, MI: Zondervan Publishing House, 1991), 30-39, 50.

Louis and other places to the south, Bounds became editor of the *St. Louis Christian Advocate* for eight years and, later, associate editor of *The Nashville Christian Advocate* for four years. The trial of his faith came while he was in Nashville, and he quietly retired to his home without even asking for a pension. His principal work in Washington, Georgia (his home), was rising at four o'clock in the morning and praying until seven o'clock. He filled a few engagements as an evangelist during the eighteen years of his life work in Washington, Georgia.

* * * * * *

W*hile I was a past*or in Atlanta, in 1905, I was informed that there was an apostolic *man of prayer in Georg*ia who would aid the church in attaining a high level in spiritual things. The next mail carried a letter asking that apostolic man – Mr. Bounds – to come to our convention for ten days of preaching. Naturally, we expected to see a man of imposing physique. But when he came, we discovered that he was only about five and a half feet tall, but in him, we met one of the greatest saints that, in our humble opinion, has appeared on the spiritual horizon in the last hundred years.

He spoke the first afternoon on prayer. No one seemed to be particularly impressed. The next morning at four o'clock, we were amazed to hear him engaged in the most wonderful prayer we have ever heard – a prayer that seemed to take in both heaven and earth. His sermons were all about prayer and heaven. Not one morning during his stay did he fail to make his prayers a great while before day (Mark 1:35). He didn't care when the other occupants of his room protested for waking them at that unheard-of hour. No man could have made more melting appeals for lost souls and backslidden ministers than did Bounds. Tears ran down his face as he pleaded for us in that room. I know of no other man on earth today who would have gone away defeated, if he had followed the same practice at the same place, in the same room. But Bounds was all powerful, all commanding, and all victorious, when once he knew his cause was just.

After that convention, we took him to our heart and never let him go. God sent him in answer to our prayer to settle and establish this writer in the things of God that are foremost and supreme – prayer, preaching, and the study of the Bible.

We were constantly with him in prayer and preaching for eight precious years. Not a foolish word did we ever hear him utter. He was one of the most intense eagles of God that ever penetrated the spiritual realm. He could not tolerate delay in rising or being late for dinner. He would often go with me to street meetings in Brooklyn, listen to the preaching, and sing those beautiful songs of Wesley and Watts with us, but reprimanded me for asking the unconverted to sing of heaven. He said, "They have no heart to sing; they do not know God, and God does not hear them. Quit asking sinners to sing the songs of Zion and the Lamb." To what mysterious order of men did Bounds belong, anyway? Have they disappeared from the world?

Few subjects create more interest in the mind of the

fervent Christian reader than the subject Bounds has named: heaven – a state, a city, and a home. He was so full of the "heavenly manna" that God produced through him that the spiritual splendor shone out of every chapter of his wonderful books.

In 1912, I wrote to him to come to Brooklyn, New York, to pray for me and my church. Here are a few excerpts from his personal letters to us at this time, which show the depths of his thought for a home in heaven.

"*Washington, July 1, 1912:* I am thinking more of going to heaven than to New York. It is far better. But it is in God's will. I would enjoy being with you. God seems to have opened the way. I will have to wait on God for New York or heaven as I am now very weak. With all love and prayer."

"*December 12 and 13, 1912:* You will pray much. I am turning to you and Chilton. One of you must help me to do the work on my manuscripts that I want finished and published. I could go to you, and then you could help me in odd times by prayer and consultation. We would then be together as long as God lets me live for His great work. We can issue the books together, and you can keep them if necessary until I die – until God's fitting time to publish."

On January 6, 1913, he writes, "Dearly Beloved: A good time praying for you. Be at it early and late. Let your mind live in the spirit of prayer. The thought of heaven is sweet. I am very weak, but will strive to work on and wait for God's time for heaven."

He was growing weaker and nearing the other shore when he wrote this letter:

"April 21, 1913: God will manage our affairs if we will be filled with His affairs. I am trying to get matters in shape for my manuscripts. I am very weak. I want to live for God, and then depart and be with Christ. I have an unspeakable desire to know the future, to see it and enjoy it, and to be there – to see and enjoy. God bless you."

The following letters I call "dying messages to one whom he loved":

"Washington, May 10, 1913: With all love and longing and prayers. God bless and keep you until eternal life. With many trials and tears, I am pressing on. I am still weak, but by sleeping in the day I can get through. When He is ready, I long for the heavenlies through Christ."

"Washington, Georgia, May 22, 1913: Yours came. I have you in prayer – at it early and trying to be at it all the day. God bless you with eternal life and hasten the day. Go out into the highways and hedges and compel them to come in. Bear your boys on your prayers to the doors of heaven. I am getting the book ready to send to England. Pray God will open the way for it – to His glory. In love and faithful prayer as my strength will allow."

He wrote one card dated June 26, 1913:

"Washington, Georgia: In prayerful sympathy

and love. Hold to the old truth – double distilled (purified and concentrated)."

The above card was the last word written to us in his own hand. On August 9, shortly before he died, his wife writes: "He was glad to hear from you but soon forgets. My physician says he will never be well again. His last message to you is characteristic: 'Tell him he is on the right track; press it. Have a high standard and hold to it.'"

Then came the telegram announcing his home-going:

"Washington, Georgia, August 24, 1913: Doctor Bounds went home this afternoon; funeral here tomorrow afternoon. – Hattie Bounds."

– Homer W. Hodge

Similar Titles

The Soul Winner, by Charles H. Spurgeon

As an individual, you may ask, How can I, an average person, do anything to reach the lost? Or if a pastor, you may be discouraged and feel ineffective with your congregation, much less the world. Or perhaps you don't yet have a heart for the lost. Whatever your excuse, it's time to change. Overcome yourself and learn to make a difference in your church and the world around you. It's time to become an effective soul winner for Christ.

As Christians, our main business is to win souls. But, in Spurgeon's own words, "like shoeing-smiths, we need to know a great many things. Just as the smith must know about horses and how to make shoes for them, so we must know about souls and how to win them for Christ." Learn about souls, and how to win them, from one of the most acclaimed soul winners of all time.

Available where books are sold

A Life for Christ, by Dwight L. Moody

In the church today, we have everything buttoned up perfectly. The music is flawless, the sermon well-prepared and smoothly delivered, and the grounds meticulously kept. People come on time and go home on time. But a fundamental element is missing. The business of church has undermined the individual's need to truly live for Christ, so much so, that only a limited few are seeing their life impact the world.

Dwight L. Moody takes us deep into Scripture and paints a clear picture of what ought to be an individual's life for Christ. The call for each Christian is to become an active member in the body of Christ. The motive is love for the Lord and our neighbor. The result will be the salvation of men, women, and children everywhere.

Available where books are sold

The Ministry of Intercession, by Andrew Murray

If the answer to prayer is so positively promised in scripture, why are there so many unanswered prayers today (often misinterpreted as a "no")? Scripture teaches us that answer to prayer depends upon certain conditions. Christ spoke of faith, of perseverance, of praying in His name, of praying in the will of God. But all these conditions were summed up in the one central statement: If ye abide in me and my words abide in you, ye shall ask what ye will, and it shall be done unto you. It becomes clear that the power to pray the effectual prayer of faith depends upon the life.

Let Andrew Murray show you what it means to live in Christ, and let his challenge for genuine intercessory prayer change your life – and the lives of those you are praying for.

Available where books are sold

Humility, by Andrew Murray

Is humility a Christlike attribute that should be pursued? And even if it should be, can genuine humility actually be attained? Often so practical in application that it is overlooked, the answer is found by studying the life and words of Christ (*whosoever will be chief among you, let him be your slave*). This little book is a loud call to all committed Christians to prove that meekness and lowliness of heart is the evidence by which those who follow the meek and lowly Lamb of God are to be known. Never mind that your initial efforts will be misunderstood, taken advantage of, or even resisted. Instead, learn from the One who *came not to be ministered unto, but to serve*. For a Christian to be alive, for the life of Christ to reign in and through us, we must be empty of ourselves, exchanging our life for His life, our pride for true, Christlike humility.

Available where books are sold

The Kneeling Christian, by Albert Richardson

Why are many Christians often defeated? Because they pray so little. Why do most men see so few brought out of darkness to light by their ministry? Because they pray so little. Why are our churches simply not on fire for God? Because there is so little real prayer.

We may be assured of this: The secret of all failure is our failure in secret prayer.

This book explores, in depth:

- God's wonder at our lack of prayer
- God's incredible promises concerning those who do pray
- God's condition for providing signs
- God's desire for earnest prayer
- God's perspective on hindrances to prayer

Available where books are sold

Absolute Surrender, by Andrew Murray

God waits to bless us in a way beyond what we expect. From the beginning, ear has not heard, neither has the eye seen, what God has prepared for those who wait for Him (Isaiah 64:4). God has prepared unheard of things, things you never can think of, blessings much more wonderful than you can imagine and mightier than you can conceive. They are divine blessings. Oh, come at once and say, "I give myself absolutely to God, to His will, to do only what God wants." God will enable you to carry out the surrender necessary, if you come to Him with a sincere heart.

Available where books are sold

www.ingramcontent.com/pod-product-compliance
Lightning Source LLC
Chambersburg PA
CBHW070146080526
44586CB00015B/1861